FILM STARS

Stars are an integral part of every major film industry in the world. In this pivotal new series, each book is devoted to an international movie star, looking at the development of their identity, their acting and performance methods, the cultural significance of their work, and their influence and legacy. Taking a wide range of different stars, including George Clooney, Brigitte Bardot and Amitabh Bachchan among others, this series encompasses the sphere of silent and sound acting, Hollywood and non-Hollywood areas of cinema, and child and adult forms of stardom. With its broad range, but a focus throughout on the national and historical dimensions to film, the series offers students and researchers a new approach to studying film.

SERIES EDITORS

Martin Shingler and Susan Smith

Madhuri DIXIT

NANDANA BOSE

BFI

THE BRITISH FILM INSTITUTE
Bloomsbury Publishing Plc
50 Bedford Square, London, WC1B 3DP, UK
1385 Broadway, New York, NY 10018, USA

BLOOMSBURY is a trademark of Bloomsbury Publishing Plc

First published in Great Britain 2019 by Bloomsbury on behalf of the British Film Institute
21 Stephen Street, London W1T 1LN
www.bfi.org.uk

The BFI is the lead organisation for film in the UK and the distributor of Lottery funds for film. Our mission is to ensure that film is central to our cultural life, in particular by supporting and nurturing the next generation of filmmakers and audiences. We serve a public role which covers the cultural, creative and economic aspects of film in the UK.

Cover design: Louise Dugdale
Cover image © *Devdas* (Sanjay Leela Bhansali, 2002), Mega Bollywood

A catalogue record for this book is available from the British Library.

Library of Congress Cataloging-in-Publication Data
Names: Bose, Nandana, author. | British Film Institute, issuing body.
Title: Madhuri Dixit / Nandana Bose.
Description: London ; New York, NY : Bloomsbury on behalf of the British Film Institute, 2019. | Series: Film stars | Includes bibliographical references, filmography, and index.
Identifiers: LCCN 2018030449 | ISBN 9781844576296 (pb) | ISBN 9781911239161 (ePDF) | ISBN 9781911239154 (epub)
Subjects: LCSH: Dixit, Madhuri. | Motion picture actors and actresses–India–Biography. | LCGFT: Biographies.
Classification: LCC PN2888.D59 B67 2019 | DDC 791.4302/8092 [B]–dc23
LC record available at https://lccn.loc.gov/2018030449

ISBN : PB: 978-93-88630-83-2

10 9 8 7 6 5 4 3 2 1

For sale in the Indian subcontinent only

Series: Film Stars

Typeset by Integra Software Services Pvt. Ltd.
Printed and bound in India by EIH Press

To find out more about our authors and books visit www.bloomsbury.com and sign up for our newsletters.

CONTENTS

ACKNOWLEDGEMENTS

I would firstly like to thank Martin Shingler, the co-editor of this series, for his patience, understanding, and support, and valuable feedback on a draft version of this manuscript. I thank him especially for keeping faith in this project since 2012 even when it nearly derailed due to an unfortunate conjunction of challenging professional and personal circumstances. I also thank Sophia Contento, Susan Smith, Nicola Cattini and Clarissa Sutherland at BFI/Palgrave Macmillan, Rebecca Willford, Project Manager at Integra Software Services, and Belinda Latchford, and Rebecca Barden, Claire Constable, and Ken Bruce at Bloomsbury Publishing for their assistance.

My thanks to the National Film Archive of India (NFAI) in Pune, in particular Aarti Kharkhanis for providing some of the images that appear in this book, and Mrs. Iyer (now retired) for facilitating access to and photocopies of archival materials. Many thanks to the University of North Carolina Wilmington's (UNCW) Office of Research and the College of Arts and Sciences for their many grant awards over the past five years that supported several field trips to/in India. Special thanks to my UNCW students, and to 'super fan', April Vuncannon for sharing her excitement and passion for all things relating to Madhuri Dixit. Prakash Jha, Rajshri's P. K. Gupta, Soumik Sen, Komal Nahta,

Chandan Arora and Deepa Gahlot shared their valuable insights during my fieldwork in Bombay spanning many summers.

Finally, this book is dedicated to my mother, Praniti Bose, a single parent who raised me, against great odds, to be a strong woman, and to whom I am indebted for her unconditional love and support.

INTRODUCTION

This monograph represents the first book-length academic study of Madhuri Dixit, one of Hindi cinema's legendary female stars. Known as the 'Dhak Dhak [Heartbeat] Girl', she was the reigning queen of popular Hindi cinema in the 1990s. Hailed as 'India's first female superstar' (Ghosh 2000: 164), 'the most valuable star in the Hindi cinema' for a brief period (Rajadhyaksha and Willemen 1999: 530), 'a one-woman army in a man-dominated industry' (Ghosh 2000: 164), the 'female Bachchan', comparing her to Amitabh Bachchan, the Hindi film industry's foremost male action hero and superstar, who enjoyed unparalleled success in the 1970s (Mehta 2011: 161) and 'Hindi cinema's most successful heroine of all time' (Sen 2014), Madhuri was the highest-paid actress in the 1990s, 'proving that heroines alone could be responsible for the commercial success of films' (Ghosh 2000: 166). Known as 'the complete Indian woman' (Sen 2014), she is celebrated for her quintessential Indian beauty, radiant smile, grace, and her riveting dance performances.

In a male-dominated film industry, her achievements are impressive. She enjoyed an enviable run at the box office, starring in a hit film every year from 1988 to 1995. When producers realised that her name on a marquee resulted in the all-important box-office opening, she began to render her heroes redundant and enjoyed a higher billing than the male lead; 'scripts like *Prem Granth* [Book of Love, 1996] [were] being specially written with her in mind' ('Madhuri Dixit: One-Up!'

1995: 32); and like the superstar Bachchan, whose name alone sold films to different territories, so did Madhuri (Ghosh 2000: 166). The *Guardian* reported that 'for several years she was the only actress who could command the same fee as male stars. She was given top billing on several pictures, and was considered so bankable that directors often paired her with lesser-known – and younger – heroes' (Goldenberg 1999). As producers inevitably bowed to her box-office potential, she raised her fees to rub shoulders with the highest-paid men – and got what she asked for. 'I'm proud I did it because it paved the path for others to follow,' she says in a recent interview.

> And when you do something groundbreaking, there's always a risk. But I think I was always clear what I wanted to be, where I wanted to be, and where I wanted women in cinema to be. So that always dictated my choices, whether it was the pricing or the choice of films, I wanted it to be the best and I thought I deserved the best. (Sen 2014)

That Madhuri managed to achieve – and, on occasion, exceed – parity in a patriarchal industry is a testament to her singular star-power.

An icon, myth, and an object of fantasy, she has been a muse for painters, poets, designers, actors, and film-makers in a collective attempt to demystify the Madhuri magic, and continues to inspire generations of young actors and dancers all over the world (as attested by the fandom of my student, April Vuncannon, who is now a trained *kathak* dancer). Madhuri's journey to stardom, hailing from an ordinary, non-*filmi*,[1] middle-class Maharashtrian family to transforming into one of Bombay cinema's greatest female stars, is nothing short of a Bollywood fairytale. She has a temple,[2] a star, a piece of waxwork, and a tribute film entitled *Main Madhuri Dixit Banna Chahti Hoon!* (*I Want to Be Madhuri Dixit!*, 2004) dedicated to her. However, despite her impressive twenty-five-year career, her indelible impact on Indian popular culture, and her continuing popularity as a transmedia celebrity there is a surprising absence of scholarship on her that this monograph seeks to redress.

Madhuri has had an unusual and distinctive career trajectory that upends pre-existing models of female stardom, by marrying at the peak of her career, withdrawing from the limelight for years, and then returning to extend her career into her early fifties by reinventing herself as a transmedia celebrity for a new generation. However, it is her unique contribution as a dancing star to Hindi cinema and popular culture that makes her stand out from other Hindi film stars, and warrants a place in this BFI Film Stars series. Known as the finest exponent of Hindi film dance, 'Dixit's dance numbers marked a redefinition of choreographic styles and radical changes in the movement vocabulary of the dancing heroine' (ibid.: 130). Sohini Ghosh posits that even in conservative films, Madhuri could 'prise open spaces for the play of women's sexuality. Even an orthodox film like *Beta* [Son, 1992] for instance is compelled to include fantasmatic (sic) interludes to accommodate the Madhuri phenomenon through its song and dance sequences' (Ghosh 2000: 167). Madhuri revelled in the subversive potential of erotic song sequences representative of spaces of resistance for Indian women surviving in a repressive society, and initiated'radical changes in popular Hindi cinema's representation of dancing bodies, especially those of its lead actresses and of female protagonists in general' (Iyer 2015: 153), thus expanding the Hindi film heroine's dance vocabulary to include movements hitherto usually attributed to the vamp.[3]

Madhuri was a zeitgeist icon of the 1990s – a star produced and shaped by her times who had the unique ability to reconcile the contradictions, conflicts and tensions of a tumultuous transitional period in modern Indian history. Studies on zeitgeist icons indicate that such stars reveal not so much what was happening socially and culturally at the time but, rather, what was coming into being or what was being left behind. 'Stars can restate, often in new and modern forms, old identities and values, as well as calling a society towards newer, and perhaps confused, emergent values and values systems' (Shingler 2012: 151). 'She was a heroine, tailor-made for contradictory times. When Madhuri Dixit started work in 1984, India was just coming to terms with the end of state control over private enterprise' (Bamzai 2008: 14), and by the time the first phase of her career ended, India was grappling with the vicissitudes of a globalised consumer culture and a rapidly transforming mediascape, precipitated by neo-liberalism. In terms of the historical context of the Hindi film industry, 'Madhuri's peak years coincided with a period of great transition in Hindi cinema' between the 1970s angry young man and 1990s romantic revival. 'She straddled the two eras with ease', producing her best work with Anil Kapoor and the superstar Khan trio: Aamir Khan, Salman Khan, and Shah Rukh Khan (ibid.: 16).

In the following section, I shall provide a brief literature review and commentary on methodology. I have adopted a multi-modal methodology that is a synthesis of several critical approaches – not overly dependent on textual analyses of star performance, it foregrounds the importance of an approach relatively uncommon in the study of Indian film stars, that is, the industrial approach, exploring the hitherto understudied yet crucial role of mentors, collaborators and industry personnel (such as director, co-star, manager, choreographer) and interpersonal relations and contacts in the construction of a Hindi film star. In short, one of the primary goals of this scholarship is to highlight the significant collaborative influences of key players in the emergence of Madhuri as a dancing star in late 1980s–early '90s popular Hindi cinema. It also seeks to emphasise dance choreographer Saroj Khan's contribution in producing the star text, for 'Dixit's body was the perfect vehicle for Khan's choreographic vision, and, together, the dancer-actress and the choreographer who achieved stardom with "Ek do teen" [One Two Three] conceptualized a new female movement vocabulary in popular Hindi cinema' (Iyer 2015: 137). Moreover, I interrogate the conjunction of political, economic, and technological factors that created the conditions for the emergence of one of the first televisual superstars of her era as

> she presided over an age that was rapidly taking the movie out of the movie hall into the living room. The increasing number of film-based programmes, featuring movie clips produced for an escalating satellite television market, could account for the centrality of song and dance numbers in her career. (Bamzai 2008: 16)

This academic study is based on archival research constituting prominent English- language film magazines, newspapers, and trade journals; primary and secondary interviews, text-based analyses, especially of star performance; extra-textual materials (publicity and promotional ephemera such as official posters), and discourse analyses of print media and fan activity. The monograph represents my current research agenda of conscientiously writing women into the historiography of Indian cinema; to record and recognise women's creative work, their talent and labour; and to treat them as fascinating and valuable texts worthy of critical thought, enquiry, and analysis. In this sense, my work is indebted to, and inspired by the groundbreaking scholarship of Neepa Majumdar (2009) on 1930s and 1940s female stars and playback singers Lata Mangeshkar and Asha Bhosle; Rosie Thomas (2015) on 1930s and 1940s stunt queen 'Fearless' Nadia; Jyotika Virdi (2003) on Meena Kumari and Dimple Kapadia; and by the pioneering interventions of Behroze Gandhy and Rosie Thomas (1991) on 1950s superstar Nargis and 'modern feminist' Smita Patil; and more recently, by Anustup Basu (2013) on the Anglo-Indian dancer/femme fatale, Helen. Following Majumdar's assertion regarding 'the centrality of innuendo as a particular rhetorical form of accessing and engaging stars' (2009: 11), this monograph highlights the saliency of scrutinising gossip, rumour, and scandal – reputation-building elements key to the construction of a star's off-screen persona. Richard Dyer's (1979/1998) groundbreaking work *Stars* informs this scholarship, specifically, his analyses of Marilyn Monroe's stardom (1986/2007), and his insights into creative labour, star vehicles, and the importance of publicity and promotions in star construction.

Usha Iyer is one of the few scholars to have critically examined the Madhuri Dixit star phenomenon. Her scholarship represents a significant intervention as she analyses the minutiae of Madhuri's dance-movement vocabulary and performance style, contending that the 'dancer-actress engenders a distinctive mode of performance that alters relations between narrative and spectacle and suggests a different model for understanding female agency and the authorship of star texts' (2015: 132). Ajanta Sircar makes a convincing argument in asserting that Madhuri navigated her route to stardom by capitalising on the increasing importance and visibility of the music segment (via the song and dance spectacle) made possible by the new audio-visual technologies of mass culture (2011: 119). Monika Mehta (2011), in her seminal work on censorship in Hindi cinema, discusses the controversy involving the raunchy song lyrics and dance sequence of 'Choli ke Peeche Kya Hai' (What's behind the Blouse) in *Khalnayak* (*Villain*, 1993) that was memorably picturised on the dancing star. Mehta incisively locates Madhuri's unique star power thus: 'Through her spectacular dance performances, Dixit commandeered screen space in a way that seriously challenged the position of the male hero.' Irrespective of genre, her 'screen presence easily overshadowed her male costars; in the popular press, for example, the two major hits of the 1990s, *Beta* and *Raja* (King, 1995), were often referred to as *Beti* (Daughter) and *Rani* (Queen)' (Mehta 2011: 161). Sohini Ghosh argues, in the popular magazine *Zee Premiere*, that 1990s Madhuri was a transgressive cult figure (2000: 169) as she reconciled in her characters the personae of both heroine and vamp. For her, 'Madhuri's screen representation becomes the most popular embodiment of this rupture … play[ing] out women's growing disenchantment with sexual conformity along with a desire to celebrate sexual assertiveness' (ibid.: 166).

A brief explanation of how I am using the phrases 'popular Hindi cinema', 'Bombay film industry', and the contested term 'Bollywood'

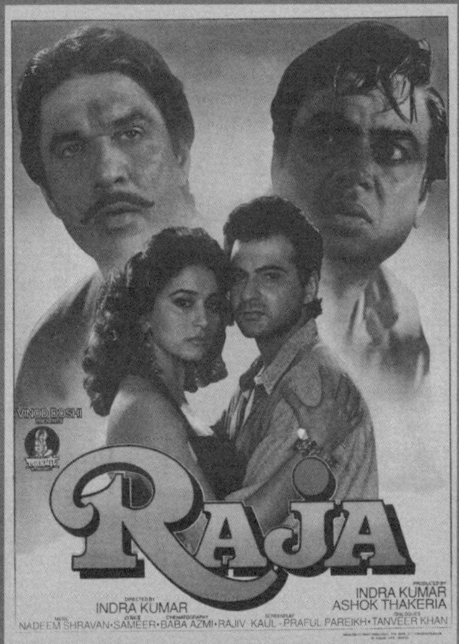

Madhuri is foregrounded in posters of *Beta* (1992) and *Raja* (1995), reflecting her star power

is important. By 'popular Hindi cinema', I allude to a certain scale of commercial film-making distinct in terms of its language, style, form, aesthetic, and narrative that has dominated the sensibilities and imagination of Indians. By no means the most prolific industry in India, as erroneously considered by many, Hindi cinema's song and dance sequences and influential star system are particularly 'popular' aspects that have determined its continued dominance and fandom, despite its chaotic film-making practices, lack of state support, threats from other regional cinema and Hollywood, and class-based prejudices that have often deemed it mindless kitsch, 'trashy' mass entertainment, symbolic of 'low taste'. When I use the phrase 'Bombay film industry', I mean Hindi cinema as a tangible, concrete, material entity, and presence, constitutive of its industrial infrastructure, labour, personnel, sites; and as a geographic location in the cosmopolitan city of Bombay, (officially renamed Mumbai in 1995), in the western state of Maharashtra. 'Bollywood', a controversial term for scholars of Indian cinema and for the Hindi film industry, has often been indiscriminately and incorrectly used to suggest that it is synonymous with 'Indian cinema', and 'Hindi cinema'. A buzzword gaining global currency primarily in the late 1990s, it is often misused ahistorically to refer to all film-making modes and styles in India, thereby ignoring the diverse and prolific regional film industries that exist within the nation. I use the term Bollywood to connote a radical shift in terms of film-making style and practices, the material and creative imbrication of the South Asian diaspora, and its global audiences, circulation, and exhibition. In this monograph, Bollywood implies a dominant culture industry (inclusive of cinema) too, with its thriving cult of celebrity, that emerged at a particular historical period in Bombay cinema as a corollary of early 1990s economic liberation and globalisation.

This final section offers an overview of the chapters that constitute the monograph. Chapter 1 contends that Madhuri's star phenomenon should be examined in terms of a collaborative process of assemblage involving several influential (predominantly male) mentors, especially foregrounding the critical role of her dance choreographer, Saroj Khan, and the considerable labour expended in the 'star-making' process to manufacture Madhuri's 'sexiness' through dance movements and costuming. As Madhava Prasad notes,

> The value deriving from a star persona is part rent and part profit. From the star's perspective, his/her body is a source of rent, since its principal quality, charisma, *is coded as a possession that he/she is 'born with', notwithstanding the work that goes into producing it*. From the perspective of the film-makers, the payment of rent enables the exploitation of this 'ground' in profit-making ventures. (2014: 141; emphasis added by author)

I seek to foreground the work involved in producing her stardom; to unpack and deconstruct the finished product a star appears to be for audiences. For Prasad, 'the star persona … accumulates within itself attributes that are specific to various instances of performance, as well as various value-laden associations deriving from personal history' (ibid.). I aim to demonstrate the importance of Madhuri's off-screen persona by scrutinising the precise nature of these 'value-laden associations from her personal history' and how they have shaped her stardom and career while considering issues of class, education, and reputation.

Chapter 2 explores the complicated relationships between new technology, music, marketing, and female stardom. The video-cassette boom and the exponential growth of private television heightened the importance of film-based song and dance sequences, and *filmi* music for the box-office success of a film, and the stars (like Madhuri) featured in these sequences gained unprecedented visibility and exposure as these segments were re-edited into music videos that were then endlessly played (almost on loop) on a plethora of newly available private cable and satellite channels. Madhuri's starry ambitions fortuitously aligned themselves with the exponential demand for music- and dance-based entertainment as televisual content. She became one of the first televisual superstars of her generation as a result of the popularity of her often erotic *filmi* song and dance performances that found platforms for mass dissemination through new music technologies and companies, and the growing importance of film-based marketing. In this sense, Madhuri is examined as a zeitgeist icon whose stardom is facilitated by the advent of audio-visual technological innovations, and reflects the political and gendered predilections of her tumultuous era.

Chapter 3 closely analyses Madhuri's performances as a dancing star in films that functioned as star vehicles while situating them within the broader industrial discourse on the danseuse. Aside from being an extensive and exhaustive textual study of her dance, it is distinctive from paltry extant scholarship as it repudiates the popular assumption that Madhuri was 'born' a naturally gifted on-screen dancing star by foregrounding her star labour and challenges of mastering specific complex dance routines and techniques; numerous adjustments and a steep learning curve that accompanied her arduous transformation into a legendary cinematic dancing star from a classically trained dancer. It also discusses the seminal role that costuming and fashion, specifically showcased in song picturisations, have played in shaping her stardom.

Chapter 4 examines the millennial reinvention of the polysemic Madhuri text transitioning from a film star to a transmedia celebrity, wherein dance continues as a salient leitmotif. It explores how she is adapting and exploiting the relatively new phenomenon of millennial celebrity culture, and responding to the singular challenges of an ageing celebrity whose stardom is no longer primarily dependent on cinema. The added pressure of maintaining a high profile and visibility is managed by her young corporate team, who strategise her social-media usage to expand her youth fan base. It considers the role of reality television as one of the entertainment industries engendering Madhuri's millennial reinvention. No longer just a film star, she has developed an expansive brand by taking advantage of the popularity of the reality-television genre and the endless possibilities that the virtual, online world of dance offers. Her innovative, imaginative, and diverse use of the internet and social media necessitates the radical reconfiguration of the discursive practices of stardom.

1 INDIA'S 'DHAK DHAK [HEARTBEAT] GIRL': RISE TO STARDOM

Brief biography

Madhuri Shankar Dixit was born on 15 May 1967 in a traditional Maharashtrian, middle-class family in Bombay (now Mumbai), in the western state of Maharashtra. Her father, Shankar Dixit, was an engineer, and her mother, Snehlata Dixit, who was artistically inclined, holds a Master's degree in music, although her first love was dance. She has three older siblings, Bharati, Rupa, and Ajit. As a child, she and her sister Rupa learnt the classical dance form of *kathak*, Madhuri winning a National Talent Scholarship at the age of eleven. She participated in elocution and dance competitions, and acted in school and college plays. She recalls a happy childhood, growing up in J. P. Nagar, a modest suburb of Andheri, and having fun even though they did not own much. She reminisces being 'totally dependent on her parents,' and leading 'a very sheltered protected life' as she was the youngest in the family (Biswas 1992).

While Madhuri was in her twelfth standard at Divine Child High school, Govind Moonis, a family friend who worked as a scriptwriter at Rajshri Productions, felt she was an appropriate choice for a debutante role in their forthcoming film, *Abodh* (*Innocent*, 1984), starring the Bengali actor Tapas Paul. Moonis approached her family, after speaking with his employers, and since 'the Rajshree (sic) people [were] known for their clean films' (Arora 1989), they agreed, but not before asking permission from her mother's orthodox family in Ratnagiri. Once her parents met Tarachand Barjatya of Rajshri Productions, they were appeased as it was 'a simple and sweet role, nothing controversial' (Rane 2010: 22). She decided to shoot the film after she had taken her school-leaving exams, since her parents wanted her to complete her education (ibid.), and then start her career at the age of sixteen. Unfortunately, *Abodh* was a disastrous debut. The *Screen* review titled 'insipidly recycled romance', described the film as 'incredibly dull', 'sterile', and 'so wholesome it is almost bland and tasteless', making passing reference to 'the new pretty face of Madhuri Dixit making her debut as the heroine … who makes a pretty foil for her glum groom' (1984: 4). It noted that the lead pair's 'chemistry somehow fails to create the right reaction, both going through the motions without much depth or conviction and losing viewer interest as a consequence' (ibid.). However, as Madhuri did not have any 'burning ambition to become an actress', she treated her failed debut as a 'passing phase and went to microbiology' (Arora 1989), joining Parle College in Bombay while acting in two more films, *Awara Baap* (*Vagrant Father*, 1985), and *Swati* (1986).

The much-recounted, inspirational story of an epic struggle during her early career is an integral part of the Madhuri Dixit myth and star phenomenon. As an outsider from a non-*filmi* family, she made the rookie mistake of accepting bit roles in B-grade films and had the dubious distinction of surviving a string of five successive failures – *Awara Baap, Swati, Manav Hatya* (*Murder of Men*, 1986), and *Hifaazat* (*Protect*, 1987). When her sixth film *Dayavaan* (*Merciful*, 1988) flopped too, she was labelled with the 'jinx it' moniker ('Heartbreaks …' 1989: 28). It was after these failures that she felt 'hurt' and 'small' and 'took up the challenge' to succeed in the industry (Arora 1989). She recalls the 'anger' within her: 'I couldn't accept the fact that what I had finally decided to do, was not working out. I was absolutely determined deep down to prove everybody wrong and myself right'

Debut film *Abodh* (1984), which failed at the box office

(Biswas 1992), which she emphatically did four years later in 1988 with N. Chandra's *Tezaab* (*Acid*), which made her an 'overnight celebrity. A star was born' ('Heartbreaks …' 1989: 28). It was the much-awaited 'turning point' in her burgeoning career after which her 'career graph started climbing upward' (Travasso 1990: 43).

Thereafter, she consistently delivered a box-office hit for eight successive years from 1988 to 1995, an unparalleled feat for a female star in the Bombay industry – *Ram Lakhan* (1989), *Dil* (*Heart*, 1990), *Saajan* (*Lover*, 1991), *Beta* (1992), *Khalnayak* (1993), *Hum Aapke Hai Kaun …!* (*Who Am I to You*, 1994; henceforth referred to by its acronym *HAHK*), featuring fourteen song and dance sequences. The last mentioned was Madhuri's most successful film in terms of box-office revenue and cultural impact, winning her her third *Filmfare* Best Actress Award and first ever *Screen* award for Best Actress, in the year *Screen* instituted its awards ('Madhuri Dixit: "They're Too Precious"' 1997: 4). It established her as a Hindi film legend, leading to more films centred around her stardom, with co-starring actors relegated to second billing such as in *Raja*, her next hit film in 1995. Throughout her early career she was compared to the then-reigning superstar Sridevi in a media-manufactured rivalry, while inevitably, from the mid-1990s, as she approached her thirties, she was either habitually written off or married off by the media, who were exasperated by her refusal to relinquish the mantle of top female star by dutifully tying the knot. Yash Chopra's 1997 *Dil to Pagal Hai* (*The Heart Is Crazy*, henceforth abbreviated to *DTPH*) was dubbed a 'comeback' as younger actresses challenged her position, while she received critical acclaim in arguably her finest role as Ketki in Prakash Jha's feminist film *Mrityudand* (*Death Sentence*, 1997).

When Madhuri tied the knot on 17 October 1999 in an arranged marriage to Dr Sriram Madhav Nene, an Indo-American cardiovascular surgeon, fluent in Marathi and, like her, an upper-caste, Konkanasth Brahmin, which was considered a 'respectable' alliance, the *Guardian* reported, to tens of millions of south Asian men, the sense of betrayal was so great that it was as if they had been jilted at the altar. Madhuri Dixit, the reigning diva of Hindi cinema for much of the 90s, had married another … . To say that Ms Dixit has broken every male heart in the country – not to mention Pakistan and the south Asian diaspora – is to render prosaic an attachment so profound that it is at once real and imaginary, intimate and public (Goldenberg 1999).

After her marriage, she relocated first to Gainesville, Florida and then to Denver, Colorado, consequently giving up her career to become a house wife and mother of two sons, Arin and Raayan born in 2003 and 2005 respectively. The first phase of her career ended in 2002 with the critically acclaimed film, *Devdas*.

Away from the greasepaint for five years, she made her 'comeback' in 2007 with Yash Raj Studios' *Aaja Nachle* (*Come, Dance!*) in 2007, while making several sporadic trips to India, and guest appearances on Indian media (primarily as a reality-television judge) until her permanent return to the country in October 2011. Subsequently, Madhuri has defied convention to re-create herself as a multimedia entrepreneurial celebrity in middle age by her skillful negotiation of career and family life, and of ageing; clever exploitation of the internet and social media; her acquisition of 'super-fans'; involvement in advertising and sponsorship, charity and campaigning; and her more recent (largely feminist) films, *Gulaab Gang* (*Pink Gang*, 2014) and *Dedh Ishqiya* (*One and a Half Romance*, 2014).

Madhuri was awarded the Padma Shri, the nation's fourth-highest civilian award, by the Government of India in 2008. In March 2011, Madhuri was honoured with a *Filmfare* Special award on completion of twenty-five years in Hindi cinema. In June 2012, a star in the Orion constellation was named after Madhuri by a group of thirteen members of The Empress Fanpage, including my student April Vuncannon, who presented her with the 'star' certificate from the Star Foundation in Mumbai ('Star in Her Name' 2012: 1). She has received six

Filmfare Awards, four for Best Actress, one for Best Supporting Actress and one special award, and has been nominated for the *Filmfare* Award for Best Actress a record fourteen times. In 2014, Madhuri was named the most inspirational Female Bollywood Icon, a category nominated by the public, becoming the first to receive the honour instituted the previous year at the third annual Bradford Inspirational Women Awards (BIWA) in Bradford, UK. Her waxwork statue was unveiled at London's Madame Tussauds in March 2012, making her the sixth Bollywood celebrity and only the second actress after Aishwarya Rai to be so commemorated, joining Bollywood legends, Amitabh Bachchan, Shah Rukh Khan, Hrithik Roshan, and Salman Khan (*Indian Express* 7 March 2012).

1980s industrial context

In the 1980s the Bombay film industry was in crisis, a chaotic and unprofessional work environment 'pushed to the limits of what it could do with the systems it had. The scale of production was frenetic, with stars doing multiple movies at once' (Wilkinson-Weber 2014: 7). Some films took years to complete, either due to a lack of reliable sources of funding or the inability of overworked stars to commit sufficient consecutive dates to finish them (ibid.: 7). Madhuri recalls how 'disorganised' it was during her time: 'There were no bound scripts; dialogue was written on the set while we were getting dressed' (Farook 2011). The 1980s were considered 'the era of video and trashy cinema' (Ganti 2011: 81) by the film industry, 'a particularly dreadful period of filmmaking', notorious for 'cliched plots and dialogues, excessive violence, garish sets, and vulgar choreography' which illustrated 'the decline in cinematic quality by the mid- to late 1980s' (ibid.).

In terms of the deeply entrenched star system of the Hindi film industry, it was a period of steady decline for Amitabh Bachchan,

Wax figure at Madame Tussauds London

coinciding with the Bofors scandal, when no one male star ruled the industry, unlike the Bachchan-dominated era of the 1970s. Shah Rukh Khan, Salman Khan, and Aamir Khan were beginning their careers as romantic heroes in the late 1980s; family audiences were put off by gratuitous violence in the notorious 'rape–revenge' cycle of films, and had retreated from the increasingly shabby environs of theatre halls; and action hero-driven 'multi-starrer' *masala* films enjoyed popularity. Thus, late 1980s popular Hindi cinema proffered limited, one-dimensional, clichéd supporting roles for women; only the song and dance, and comic sequences yielded a few 'spectacular' opportunities for heroines to make a lasting visual impact by showcasing their talent for dancing, physical comedy, and even acting.

Mentors and collaborators

For a rank 'outsider' like Madhuri, negotiating a seemingly impenetrable web of intensely close kinship, familial, and interpersonal ties binding the semi-feudal industry without influential mentors would have been a near-impossible feat. This amorphous industrial structure has thwarted many starry aspirations and fledgling careers. Therefore, I contend that Madhuri's star phenomenon should be examined in terms of a collaborative process of assemblage involving several influential male mentors and personnel (namely, the director/producer and 'star-maker' Subhash Ghai, producer Boney Kapoor and his brother, the star Anil Kapoor, and her manager Rakesh Nath), and creative collaborators (choreographer Saroj Khan) who took a keen personal interest in the advancement of her career, and closely collaborated with each other to relaunch, nurture, and produce a star who eventually became short-hand for 'Bollywood' glamour, box-office success and mass appeal. The first section of this chapter adopts an undervalued and neglected approach to the construction of Hindi film stardom that emphasises the extra-textual agencies shaping star careers by foregrounding the creative and industrial labour of Madhuri's coterie of trusted collaborators/associates (director–manager–co-star–choreographer–hairdresser) during her protracted period of 'struggle' that transformed the 'ordinary' Madhuri into an 'extraordinary' star.

The role of the self-proclaimed star-maker and director Ghai, successful at the box office for two decades, from the 1980 release *Karz* (*Debt*) to the 1999 *Taal* (*Rhythm*), is particularly significant. A product of the prestigious Film and Television Institute of India (FTII), Ghai began his career as an actor in 1970 and moved successfully to direction in 1976 with *Kalicharan*. In 1983, he became an independent producer, establishing his company Mukta Arts, and was one of the leading producer-directors of the 1980s, helming many successful films (Mehta 2011: 160). While Madhuri was shooting in Kashmir for Sohanlal Kanwar's film *Awara Baap*, Ghai, location hunting for his forthcoming film *Karma* (1986), visited the set and Madhuri was introduced to him by her resourceful hairdresser, Khatoon, as a 'good dancer'. He asked if she would be interested in performing a dance in *Karma* and, when she agreed, shot a couple of screen tests (performing 'one emotional scene, one comic act, a song and dance ...') in his Bombay office. She recalls being very nervous about these tests, but when Ghai informed her that he wanted to relaunch her in a leading role, requesting that she stop all the bit roles, and immediately signed her for *Uttar Dakshin* (*North South*, 1987) and *Ram Lakhan* (1989), she knew that it was the first step towards building a successful career (Sanjay 1986: 19). Subsequently, the dance she was supposed to perform in *Karma* was scrapped.

Ghai placed a six-page full-length advertisement in the leading trade paper *Screen* on 17 January 1986 relaunching her, and the rest is, indeed, history.[1] The advertisement read: 'Time creates history. The girl who could not succeed till 1985 ... Becomes superstar in 1986 ... Her name is Madhuri ... Madhuri, the confidence of leading filmmakers who signed her for their forthcoming films' (3–9). It proclaimed that six producers (including himself) – Yash Chopra, Shashi Kapoor, Bapu, Shekhar Kapoor, Boney Kapoor, K. C. Bokadia, and N. N. Sippy (in the order mentioned in the advertisement) – had signed Madhuri for their forthcoming projects, giving her flagging career a much-needed boost and raising her visibility.

There was considerable press coverage of her relaunch, which was treated as nothing short of a miracle for an actress who had been so nearly written off by the industry but was now 'a dark horse racing towards the goal post' (Sanjay 1986: 19). According to Deepa Gahlot, 'if a commercially successful director of Ghai's caliber, who was at his peak, decided to re-launch an actress, then success was assured. He gave Madhuri confidence, starting from Rajshri films (which would have taken her nowhere) to the A-list' (personal communication, 26 June 2013).

However, despite Ghai's high-profile promotional stunt, the flops continued, although after Ghai had signed her on for *Uttar Dakshin* and *Ram Lakhan* (which subsequently proved a box-office hit), Madhuri did continuously receive offers to work on big-banner films as a result of her influential mentor/godfather's confidence in her talent, and her new-found visibility[2] (Sircar 2011: 187). Thus, an actress was reborn as a star thanks to a promotional gimmick that eventually paid off.

During the intervening period of struggle from the appearance of the advertisement till she proved herself in her first hit film *Tezaab* in 1988, that she refers to as 'her acid test' (Mohamed 1997: 64), there were cynical print-reports declaring that even a year later she was yet to arrive (Hedge 1987: 9); describing her as 'a "paper tiger", until N. Chandra gave her a massive build-up during the making ofTezaab … [by calling] her the reincarnation of Madhubala, an echo of Meena Kumari' (Mukherjee 1990: 31). Additionally, Ghai, dubbed 'the showman who made Madhuri what she is today', (John

1993b: 21) continued to aggressively promote his protégé to film-makers, producers, and influential male actors, and expressed great confidence in her star potential, even when producers' interest in her fluctuated between 1986 and 1988. He is famously quoted as saying: 'Madhuri is a volcano of talent. A highly talented girl, she possesses a finesse in dance, singing and acting. Just wait for 1987. She will be a superstar' (Sanjay 1986: 19). His prophecy came true, albeit not in 1987 but the following year with *Tezaab*. History did vindicate his prediction that all Madhuri needed was one big hit and thereafter nobody could stop her (Ghai 1988). According to him, she had 'a sound grasp of music and dance', emoted well and 'was improving with every schedule'. She was 'one of the very few conscientious girls around in films … and her biggest asset [was] her discipline and dedication, her good behavior [having] stood her in good stead even when her films failed' (ibid.).

Madhuri, in turn, agreed that it was 'necessary to have a big name backing you [...] in the industry' and that Ghai's keen interest and involvement in her career proved pivotal (Iyer 1986: 45), acknowledging 'Subhashji for actively promoting' her and for being the first to sign her on for two films together. She recollects that 'it was only after he signed [her] that the other producers came forward' (Arora 1989). He also advised her 'properly and correctly' and did not take advantage of her. In her words, 'Subhashji is someone I owe a lot to' (Biswas 1992). Besides his crucial role as adviser and promoter, Ghai taught her 'how to face the camera, which angle to look at, how to look, the works …' (Rane 2010: 25). She says she learnt from him 'how to enter a frame, how to stand in front of the camera, and how never to be relaxed', as well as 'how one should be intensely professional' (Kalarikal 1996: 51).

To his credit, he did not stop promoting her even after she had achieved stardom as she was cast on Ghai's recommendation in Jha's critically acclaimed film *Mrityudand*, arguably her most impressive performance (P. Jha, personal communication, 21 June 2013). Thus,

Madhuri's name is closely linked with Ghai, following in the tradition of famous director–star collaborators such as Nargis and Raj Kapoor, and Waheeda Rehman and Guru Dutt. 'Such associations emerged as a result of the family structure that characterised Bombay cinema, making director–star and star pairings a frequent occurrence' (Shingler 2012: 115). Ghai also suggested Rakesh Nath (aka 'Rikkuji') for the position of secretary and manager, thus initiating a fruitful and lengthy professional relationship that would turn out to be indispensable for both parties.

The contribution of her long-time secretary Rakesh Nath, whom she shared with co-star Anil Kapoor, cannot be overstated. It was one of the longest star–secretary relationships in an industry notorious for shortlived, acrimonious relations between stars and managerial staff, the role of the secretary/manager in the Hindi film industry consequently being understudied and overlooked in extant scholarship on Indian cinema. As Tejaswini Ganti notes, if an actress advocates for herself and directly negotiates with industry personnel then she runs the risk of producers getting the wrong idea that she is desperate and brazen. Instead, it is the secretary who goes around to producers with the actress's portfolio and secures contacts (2011: 134). Thus, the key role of the secretary is to advocate on his client's behalf so that she is always protected and does not expose herself and make herself vulnerable in a masculinised space.

Rikku was an ambitious man, described in trade papers as 'a dynamo of action and ideas' who never took no for an answer and said anything was possible if you had the will … moving like lightning, making others work till the job is done … a great provider' (John 1993a: 27). A man from humble beginnings who, as a boy in Hoshiarpur, Punjab, had always dreamt of becoming a successful Hindi film producer, he started out modestly as secretary to two minor actresses, Ranjeeta and Salma Agha before joining Anil Kapoor as his secretary (ibid.: 21).

Nath recollects Madhuri's hairdresser Khatoon, who she shared with Agha, first mentioning her. On seeing Madhuri for the first time, he thought she was 'a bit on the thin side', but still felt she had potential ('Has Sanjay Changed Madhuri?' 1993: 9). Over the years, Rikkuji became more like an influential family member, steering her career, handling everything from deciding on her films and dates to her interviews and photo-sessions (Mukherjee 1990: 33). For Madhuri, who admits she wasn't 'business-minded', business acumen being essential for succeeding in the industry, it was a 'boon' having her secretary around because he handled the various branches of filmdom, distribution, selling, exploitation of territories, and finance, about which she was ignorant. While she was learning the ropes, she also let Rikkuji do all the talking because she 'did not want to rub anyone in the industry the wrong way by saying anything out of place' ('How Success Has Changed Madhuri Dixit' 1991: 17).

He was also responsible for the number of films starring Anil Kapoor and Madhuri, 'cleverly mixing her career with that of his other boss' as it was easy to coordinate their respective schedules. When she was trying to get a foothold in the industry, Rikku found it much easier to convince his already established star client, Anil Kapoor, to act opposite a rank newcomer. Then when their film *Tezaab* became 'such a super-duper hit and was followed by another hit "Ram Lakhan," producers started queueing (sic) up' for them (ibid.: 19). Kapoor recollects that sharing his secretary Rikku with her led to considerable speculation: 'Maybe we did recommend her for films like *Prem Pratigyaa* [*Promise of Love*, 1989] but it wasn't as if we were trying to push some *faltu* (useless) heroine. Madhuri had magic and she proved everyone wrong …' (Nilesh 1996: 29–30).

A string of failures and questionable film choices during the early years strikes a discordant note in the star–secretary relationship, which was conveniently attributed to her lack of experience and 'insider' knowledge of the industry. Nath's wife, Reema Rakesh Nath, wrote some of the film scripts starring Madhuri such as *Sailaab* (*Flood*, 1991), *Saajan*,

Yaraana (*Friendship*, 1995), *Aarzoo* (*Desire*, 1999), and *Hum Tumhare Hain Sanam* (*I Am Yours, My Love*, 2002), three of which were box-office failures. The press claimed Madhuri was too dependent on Nath, suggesting that she was manipulated and controlled by him; 'a puppet in the hands of her secretary', misled into starring in his failed home productions (Mukherjee 1990: 33). Khalid Mohamed reporting for *Filmfare* in 1998 observed that 'Rikoo (sic), her trusty secretary, was often socked by showbizwallas. He [was] squarely blamed for the debacles of his self-produced *Yaarana* and *Mohabbat* [*Romance*, 1997]' (26–34).

The perception of Rikku based on media reportage was of a man who was destroying Madhuri's career, based on its extensive reportage of the brouhaha over conflicting dates, his sudden withdrawal from projects and bailing on producers leading to charges of arrogance and unprofessionalism. Madhuri, on her part, felt her naïveté lay behind these complications, her secretary bearing the brunt of the criticism for the fact that she was unaccustomed to the ways of filmdom.

However, instead of blaming Madhuri for unprofessionalism, the negative press was deflected towards the 'high-handedness' of the controversial figure of the 'shrewd star secretary'; represented in the press as a conniving Machiavellian figure quietly working behind the scenes to forge a career for his client. Madhuri acknowledges that she owed a lot to him as she had always been 'sheltered from the harsher realities of struggle' ('Heartbreaks …' 1989: 28). She trusted him implicitly and had no reason to doubt him because her career was sailing smoothly, so she continued to affirm that 'she had full faith in him' (Sanjay 1988: 25). Nath played multiple roles as her gatekeeper, safety net, buffer, fall guy, all rolled into one. A different perspective is gleaned from speaking with industry insiders on Nath. According to Gahlot,

> Madhuri handled her career very well. Rikku Rakesh Nath had a big role to play in this – selecting the roles, making sure she was associated with the right

banners. He wasn't just a secretary, just a person who would say 'yes, madam, no madam.' He steered her career in the right path and towards what he thought were good projects and he did a really good job. He was an assiduous manager, keeping undesirable people away from her. Very few actresses had such a dedicated manager for such a long period. (personal communication, 26 June 2013)

The trade analyst Komal Nahta concurs, noting that Nath 'selected films well, being very particular about which films were signed' (personal interview). According to Ghai, Rikku was 'Madhuri's anchor, her front man'. She believed in him and ceded control to him. Ghai gave him 'full marks for being so loyal and sincere to her' and, unlike some media reporters, he did not believe she had been exploited (Pammi 1999b: 36–40).

The brothers, Anil and Boney Kapoor, played a crucial role in promoting and supporting Madhuri's career, and recommending her to producers in the early years. Boney Kapoor was a well-known producer who, like his brother, discerned star quality in Madhuri and felt she was 'very confident' and 'very determined' to succeed (Chopra 2011a: 46). His younger brother, Anil, best known internationally for his role as the shady quiz anchor in Danny Boyle's *Slumdog Millionaire* (2008), frequently co-starred in numerous films throughout her career, such as *Parinda* (*Pigeon*, 1989), *Ram Lakhan*, *Beta*, *Pukar* (*Call*, 2000) to name just a few. He met Madhuri for the first time on the sets of *Chameli ki Shaadi* (*Chameli's Marriage*, 1986), and their first film together was *Hifaazat*. Her former hairdresser, Khatoon, had introduced them (Nilesh 1996: 28). Initially, Kapoor was strongly opposed to Madhuri being cast as he thought 'she looked too *ganwaar*' (rustic) but she proved him wrong. He is quoted in a 1987 *Star & Style* article: 'Madhuri is a very talented girl and I personally think she was better than me in *Hifaazat*' (6–19 November: 24). A few years later in 1990, Kapoor, convinced she would 'carve a niche for herself', confirmed that he promoted Madhuri … by signing five films opposite her. I was the first major hero to do so when she was still to make it, falling in with Subhash Ghai's and Boney's plans to promote her. We gave her the first big boost, the rest she managed on her own talent and steam … ('Anil Kapoor: "They Are Jealous!"' 1990: 20)

Since male stars like Kapoor enjoy considerable clout in the patriarchal Bombay film industry wherein kinship relations and family contacts (rather than talent or hard work) often make all the difference, his endorsement carried immense weight and could galvanise the nascent career of a relatively unknown actress, because, as Gandhy and Thomas remind us, historically 'male stars have by far the highest "value," commanding at least double what comparable female stars earn, and a female star's value is determined largely by which stars are prepared to work with her' (1991: 109).

For Madhuri, Kapoor was 'an exemplary co-star' (Mohamed 1997: 62) who was 'highly encouraging' because he too had struggled during his initial years (Kalarikal 1996: 51). At a time when most heroes were unwilling to work with her, he repeatedly signed films opposite her ('Heartbreaks …' 1989: 28). He was supportive not only in aggressively promoting her career by signing her on, and using his influence and contacts, but he also helped her develop into a better performer by giving her useful suggestions on how to emote in difficult scenes. In those early years, Madhuri admits she was 'inhibited' and 'shy' because she had little training, facing the camera for the first time in *Abodh*. Since she had never considered a 'prospective acting career', she was learning how to act 'by trial and error, by what [she] would call practical experience' (Mohamed 1997: 62). According to Kapoor, the scene where Madhuri gets hysterical in *Tezaab* marked her metamorphosis. He believes that it wasn't just one 'Ek Do Teen' that launched her but it was her entire work in the film that made her a star (Nilesh 1996: 30). Madhuri's on-screen chemistry with Kapoor, with whom she was paired sixteen times, made them one of Hindi cinema's most popular screen couples.[3] For film-maker Chandan Arora, whose debut feature, *Main Madhuri Dixit Banna Chahti Hoon*, was a tribute to Madhuri's stardom, the Kapoor–Dixit *jodi*'s (couple's) films were always keenly anticipated, recollecting screenwriters' desire to 'write the next mature love story for them' (personal communication, 4 July 2013).

Madhuri's expanded star entourage was comprised of make-up artists and dress designers, such as Anna Singh and Leena Daru, and later in the mid-1990s, the famed Manish Malhotra, synonymous with Indian *haute couture*. Madhuri's hairdresser, Khatoon, was occasionally mentioned in press interviews as a key person in initiating contact with Ghai, Nath, and Anil Kapoor – a useful go-between, buffer, match-maker, confidante, who facilitated connections on behalf of her star client. As Clare Wilkinson-Weber points out –

> The hairdresser is rarely only a hairdresser, but instead does a multitude of tasks for the star. She is neither an intimate nor a relative … she mediates between star and dressman, star and designer, or indeed star and anyone else the heroine wants or needs to deal with by proxy … The hairdresser is also an important booster and confidant for the star, sometimes being entrusted with more complex secrets, such as carrying messages to and from actors in illicit relationships… She is also the only professional woman allowed free and easy access to a female star's trailer, and acts as her official dresser since there isn't anyone formally assigned to perform that job. (2014: 75)

With the rising importance of song and dance segments in post-1980s Hindi cinema, the dance choreographer's contribution became increasingly valuable, further elaborated in Chapters 2 and 3. Saroj Khan, who holds the record for the most number of Filmfare Awards for Best Choreography, played a vital role in making Madhuri 'sexy' by giving her a dramatic image make-over, and by expertly honing her now-acclaimed dancing skills. At the time, there was no one who could compete with the 'pleasantly-plump dance director who [...] had all the big names in the industry dance to her tune. From Nanda, Waheeda to Mumtaz, to the present-day, Rekha, Sridevi and Madhuri, all [...] matched steps with the 5-ft dynamite (sic)' (Jagirdhar-Saxena 1989).

Contrary to popular belief, Madhuri had divulged in an interview to *Movie* magazine that she 'had to work hard at being sexy' (Kothari 1995: 28). Initially perceived as an acne-prone, skinny, girl-next-door type, dismissed by the media as 'a stick' ('Indra Kumar: "They Said I Was Crazy to Sign Aamir!"' 1990: 48), and 'a slip of a girl, thin, dusky, hesitant smile' (Arora 1989), she gradually transformed before the camera into an extraordinarily skilled dancer and a voluptuous, photogenic on-screen performer, thus foregrounding 'the stars-as-ordinary and the stars-as-special' contradiction underpinning the phenomenon of stardom (Dyer 1998: 43). A vital part of that physical transformation was manufacturing/constructing her 'missing' sex appeal and industriously working on her attractiveness and 'look', helping her to accrue star value.

Khan played a crucial role in fashioning Madhuri's sexy image by introducing provocative body movements, postures, and gestures that included suggestively lifting up her skirt, the so-called *jhatkas* and *matkas* (provocative gyrations) to her dance repertoire, and by frequently selecting cleavage-enhancing, padded, tight-fitting *cholis* (blouses) accentuating the bust and below-the-waist *ghagra* (skirts) that became an integral part of the Madhuri figuration. Such tight-fitting, revealing costumes amplifying the star's bosom, and usually captured in close-ups, were accessorised with heavy traditional jewellery and ornate *bindis* (dots). Enhancing Madhuri's raunchiness, Khan introduced seductive facial and coy eye expressions – pouting, lip-biting, smiling, and teasing – to her expressive range to tremendous effect. According to Gahlot,

> Saroj Khan had a big role to play in both Sridevi's and Madhuri's careers. She choreographed them well. She actually gave them their expressions,

Madhuri's dancing-star persona and trademark costuming captured on the official Hindi poster of *Khalnayak* (1993)

movements. She was the kind of woman who would say: 'pick up your *ghagra*, lower your blouse, let them see what you have.' She brought out the sexiness in Madhuri which she did not have. In her initial pictures she had no style, just a simple, Marathi middle-class girl who suddenly in 'Dhak Dhak' and 'Choli ke Peechey' became this confident, well-endowed actress. That Saroj Khan had a lot to do with. She picked the costumes. She had them look sexy. And not just for Madhuri, even the people dancing in the background. She had the *namak* ('salt'). (personal communication, 26 June 2013)

The 'respectable' star with a 'boring love life': Off-screen persona, class, reputation

In late 1988, after Madhuri had become an overnight sensation with the success of *Tezaab*, the now-defunct popular film magazine, *Star & Style* queried:

Madhuri … has a boring love life and a touch-me-not attitude. Does she enjoy her goody-goody reputation? "Oh I love it! I don't indulge in any kind of nonsense. I come from a traditional family. It is in my nature. I'm not pretending to be that way … ." (1988b: 67–9)

Nearly a decade later in 1997, when film journalists were still asking her to defend her 'boring' off-screen image, she posed an interesting rhetorical question that continues to form the essence of star publicity and media practices: 'Isn't it tragic that if someone has a well-balanced, healthy attitude, we consider them boring? Why should only the sizzling and the scandalous sorts make news?' (Pillai 1997: 51). A fairly thoroughgoing articulation of the interplay between the professional and personal life engenders star identity. This forthcoming section examines how Madhuri's 'boring' off-screen persona offset her 'sexy' on-screen image and crucially contributed to a lengthy career and stable moral reputation that were inextricably tied to societal and industrial assumptions about class and education.

'With the emergence of the star, the question of the player's existence outside his/her work in films entered discourse … . The private lives of the stars emerged as a new site of knowledge and truth' (DeCordova cited in Gledhill 1991: 26). Mediated gossip, rumour and scandal articulate the private lives of stars and thus these elements are seminal to any rigorous analyses of individual film stars and the phenomenon of stardom in general. Paul McDonald suggests that

> authenticity of gossip … has little bearing on its effects, with oft-repeated but proven to be false accusations becoming core components of a star's enduring image … the significance of star scandals lies in the way that it divides (sic) a star's private life into two distinct components: 'a publicly controlled private-image and a hidden secret private-image' (39). While the former (i.e., a 'private' life) is intended for public consumption, the latter (i.e., the real private life) is kept off-limits and fiercely protected. Once exposed, the private life becomes a star's 'private' life and a significant part of their publicity and persona. (cited in Shingler 2012: 144)

Neepa Majumdar reminds us how in the 1930s,

> in the unofficial mode of stardom, gossip had primarily to do with issues of female sexuality, the boundaries of private and public, and notions of the respectability of the new medium, all of which were integrally tied to conceptions of gender and class. (2009: 38)

The nature of gossip circulated about female Hindi film stars during the 1980s–90s did not significantly alter, although over decades gossip has become decidedly an official site and mode of stardom, with a surfeit of scandalous and gossipy content published in a plethora of English-language and vernacular film, fan, lifestyle, and women's magazines (such as *Filmfare, G, Showtime, Movie, Cine*

Film magazines are ideal conduits for the dissemination of gossip, rumour, and innuendo about stars

Blitz, Stardust, Star & Style and *Screen*) that were 'generally aimed at middle-class readers, combining glossy advertisements … with salacious gossip about Bollywood and Hollywood stars' (Shingler 2012: 135). As Sircar notes, 'with the emergence of film magazines such as *G*, the 1980s actually saw a proliferation of popular journalism selling Star lives to a highly cine-literate audience' (2011: 116)

Class and regional identity

Considering Hindi cinema's long history of troubled female stars (Madhubala, Nargis, and Sridevi to name a few) from working-class families forced into the industry from a tender age to support and become the sole breadwinner for their families, Madhuri's 'non-*filmi*', middle-class family background was a significant departure from the norm, and set her apart in terms of how she was perceived by the industry and her audiences. As a way of counteracting the moral and social stigma attached to the film industry, it 'valorizes Indian middle-class norms of respectability and morality explicitly linking the moral and social status of cinema with the class backgrounds of film personnel …' (Ganti 2011: 120). This anxiety is historically connected with the industry being perceived as a morally dubious place due to its association with courtesans and prostitutes, organised crime, illegal money ('black' money), and the 'casting couch' (ibid.: 124). Hailing from an educated, upper-caste, Hindu Brahmin family, she represented a kind of middle-class respectability that was unusual and prized. She was, to quote Ganti, one of those 'girls from "good families" in the film industry' (ibid.: 121).[4] Madhuri herself was highly conscious of her middle-class upbringing and values, repeatedly and persistently emphasising her class and family in print-media interviews spanning her entire career to the point that it became tedious self-propaganda. For instance, in a 1989 *Showtime* cover feature sensationally headlined, 'The Mysterious Madhuri Dixit: Is She Hard and Ruthless?' Madhuri says, 'I am family-oriented … . It's my upbringing which is responsible for my sense of values' (Arora 1989). The same year she tells *Cine Blitz*: 'The qualities that I am most attracted to are traditional values to the point of being old fashioned' (Singh 1989: 57). Some years later, in a 1994 *Filmfare* article, Madhuri once again remarks, 'I was born into a middle class family, I believe in traditional values …' (Bharadwaj 1994: 52). Decades later, in yet another cover feature, this time in *Savvy* magazine, she is quoted as saying: 'even though we had a middle-class upbringing and didn't have much, we still had a lot of fun' (Rane 2010: 20). In fact, throughout her three-decade-long career, with unfailing consistency, like a leitmotif, she reiterated the importance of her traditional middle-class upbringing and her family – reiterations that played a crucial role in shaping and projecting a stable, and predictably consistent, off-screen persona.

Madhuri went to great lengths to preserve and protect her (and, by extension, her family's) moral reputation at a time when women were rarely seen working on film sets.[5] As she says, 'she had to deal with such taboos as good girls don't join movies and [...] didn't want anyone to point a finger at [her] parents and say, "look what they've done to their daughter's life"' (Mohamed 1997: 63). Ganti reveals that even

> at the peak of her acting career and ... almost thirty years old ... [she] frequently had her father present on the set of Dil to Pagal Hai. He paid little attention to the shoot, and sat quietly reading a book. (2011: 135)

She was not comfortable working on shoots unless someone from her family was in attendance (Travasso 1990: 44); a routine that she believes saved her from the exploitative practice of the proverbial casting couch. Insisting that her parents accompany her to film sets was her way of shielding herself from untoward sexual advances, salacious rumour-mongering, and innuendo in this patriarchal industry, with its attendant institutional, rhetorical, and discursive practices, that in contra-distinction to male stars, has obsessively focused on the private lives and morality of its female stars and actresses, rather than their professional achievements. As Behroze Gandhy and Rosie Thomas point out, 'not only is the industry unremittingly male-dominated and considered "dirty" by many, but female stars are inevitably positioned both as object of veneration and as sex object, as supremely powerful and as passive pawns of a male industry'(1991: 109).

Aside from class, I contend that her Maharashtrian regional identity played an important part in her construction as a mainstream Hindi film star in 1990s India. It becomes apparent in interviews that she is conscious of the advantage of her ethnic and regional roots, asserting that 'being Maharastrian puts [her] apart' in comparison to earlier No. 1 heroines (Kothari 1993), and declaring herself 'very proud' and pleased that she had come so far as a Maharashtrian' (Kothari 1994: 33) despite the fact that 'it was not considered good to learn dance, especially for a girl from a Maharashtrian family' (Rane 2010: 33). Writing a cover feature celebrating Maharashtra Day for *Screen* in 1993, she notes people telling her how 'after a long time a Maharashtrian girl has made it to the top in this film industry' ('Heart to Heart' 1993: 25). The film press was conscious of her ethnic community too. *Cine Blitz* refers to her as the 'little middle-class, Maharashtrian *mulgi*' (Biswas 1992); *Movie* is reminded of another Maharashtrian career woman, Lata Mangeshwar, the famous playback singer (Kothari 1993); *Savvy*'s lengthy cover feature entitled 'Mad about Madhuri' is subheadlined 'Childhood: Middle-class Values and the Marathi *Mulgi*' (Rane 2010: 33). Significantly, Madhuri spoke in fluent, non-accented Hindi diction and pronunciation as compared to the heavily accented Hindi spoken by her 'rival', the Tamilian, Sridevi, that immediately marked her as 'southern', 'marginal', and 'other' to the dominant, Hindi-speaking populace, contributing to her comedic persona.

Education and 'outsider' position

Education plays a salient role in determining class in India, 'class hierarchy [being] directly linked to education' (Majumdar 2009: 61). Madhuri's educated, non-*filmi* background tapped into film-makers' innate insecurity about the 'lack' of higher education within the industry, a source of perennial social anxiety. 'Formal higher education operates as an important measure and index of respectability for the Hindi film industry' (Ganti 2011: 144). Fixation with and desire for higher education 'can be understood as a response to the dominant stereotypes of Hindi filmmakers – as uneducated, uncouth, and unrefined' (ibid.: 144–7). Press reports referred to her as 'the girl from a middle class family, who wanted to study microbiology, and top the university' (Sanjay 1988: 23–5); noting that her 'mother … is a post graduate in classical Indian music' (Singh 1989: 57) and her father, an engineer by profession, chose to hone his English-language skills by reading *Reader's Digest* while chaperoning his daughter on film sets. Madhuri, in turn, foregrounded her predilection for academia by informing the press that she read a lot – 'everything from Sidney Sheldon and James Hadley Chase to magazines'; enjoyed spending time between shoots solving crossword puzzles (Mohamed 1997: 60), a decidedly intellectual pastime for a film star; and reminding them that she would have been a microbiologist had she not accepted Rajshri's offer to act in her debut feature: 'Acting was going to be just a hobby for me, another dimension to my personality ... I suppose, my indecisiveness about a career in academics or a career in films, had me leaning towards the latter' (Biswas 1992). Such reports of her parents' and her academic aspirations further underscored her middle-class persona, and 'respectable' social standing.

Apart from her educated background, Madhuri insistently claimed an 'outsider' status, as someone who had initially thought of acting as a passing phase or mere hobby, expecting to follow the scholarly route typical of an academically inclined middle-class family and one considered desirable and respectable. 'I had no relatives in the industry. I had given up my studies. I was a total stranger in the show world', she informed *Filmfare* (Mohamed 1997: 63). Interviews with her mother confirmed their initial trepidation about entering the film world, historically stigmatised as a morally dubious, excessive, extravagant, degenerate place: 'coming from a conservative Maharashtrian family, initially we were a little reluctant at the thought of Madhuri joining the industry. What's more we had not exactly heard redeeming things about the industry' (Divecha 1991). Even 'several blunders' that she made early in her career while negotiating the proverbial 'big, bad world of Hindi cinema' were conveniently explained away or rationalised by persistently invoking her class, 'outsider' status, and non-*filmi* background, or displaced onto the figure of her secretary, Rakesh Nath, 'the scheming brain and manipulator behind Madhuri's not-so-innocent moves' (Sanjay 1988: 24).

Managing prurient gossip and rumour

The private lives of stars, their wild indulgences, excesses, and vices, their romances and extravagant lifestyles have been the perennial fodder for gossip, rumour, and scandal,[6] capturing the romantic imagination of filmgoers worldwide. As Jyotika Virdi observes,

> Among the constituting elements of the Hindi film industry, the single most dominant group, the films (sic) stars, have a powerful grip on people's imagination, and the narratives about film stars' lives occupy film magazines and film journalism – virtually an ancillary industry. These 'star texts', supposedly based on rumor and scurrilous reporting, are marked by fascination with and admiration for the lives of the rich and famous. Female stars' lives are embedded in public discourses on love, romance, marriage, and sexuality – the traditional technologies of gender construction in Hindi cinema. (2003: 136)

Thus, historically, female stars have been (and are) vulnerable to even greater prurient public scrutiny, gossip, and scandal than their male counterparts, particularly in a traditional patriarchal society where female sexuality and chastity problematically overlap with notions of familial, communal and national honour, pride and shame. Majumdar notes:

> Gossip itself has been gendered feminine, with women as both the subject and object of the forms of unofficial knowledge associated with it. With stardom as an institution fundamentally constituted by gossip, the link between gender and stardom was thus framed by the feminized status of cinema in India and its performing women as the generalized object of gossip. (2009: 39)

Over the years, Madhuri became adept at deflecting, diffusing, and occasionally spin-doctoring smutty reports of (potential) scandals and titillating gossip with diplomacy, tact, and intelligent communication skills. A typical response from her would be:

'Honestly, I don't know what these people are talking about. I only know one affair and that is my love for my family and my work next to my family' (Ali 1986: 6). Sircar observes that, even when there were rumours 'of affairs with several men that mattered – Ghai himself, N. Chandra, even Anil Kapoor … Dixit never overtly denied them. What she did instead was to play up an "ordinariness" that would implicitly counter such allegations' (2011: 187) by projecting herself as a 'responsible' and 'disciplined' person who 'took every little thing [she did] with the utmost seriousness' (Mohamed 1997: 60); and by invoking her family values, pointing out that she would never go against her parents' wishes (Bharadwaj 1994: 52), and that her life didn't 'have any drama or fire' as she 'was born into a middle class family [and] believe[d] in traditional values' (ibid.).

She maintained a detached and dignified demeanour, rarely reacting to lascivious gossip, rumour mongering and potential scandals, or negative press reportage of which there was a surfeit during her early career. Moreover, she distanced herself from her audacious peers, believing that 'unlike other girls … having well-publicized affairs and equally publicized break-ups are not the only exciting things in life. There is so much more. But maybe others think differently so I'm labelled boring' (*Stardust*, February 1990: 67). Instead, she believed that 'discretion and dignity [were] the keywords to an actress' public image' (Singh 1989: 55). She displayed both in managing the one allegedly serious romantic liaison, extensively covered by the media, that dominated the early years of her career – her apparent affair with her co-star, Sanjay Dutt, the troubled star son of iconic actors Nargis and Sunil Dutt. After initially denying any romantic liaison with Dutt, denials which fell on deaf ears, she says she started 'taking scandal in [her] stride with a shrug of [her] shoulders' (Biswas 1992). Later in her career, she recalls that 'rumours about Sanjay and [her] did not bother [her] at all. [She] never let rumours affect [her]' (Kalarikal 1996: 53). Even the frustrated media acknowledged that she was 'the kind of woman who isn't even bothered about clearing the romantic stories reported by various magazines about her and her co-stars' (Biswas 1992). Whenever questioned about the relationship, she would decline to comment, deflect attention, or change the topic. Film magazines and newspapers duly noted 'that her mother managed her love life (according to the gossip mill, Dixit's mother singlehandedly broke up the romance between Dixit and her "nefarious" co-star Sanjay Dutt)' (Mehta 2011: 161). The veracity of this affair was never corroborated by either side, the exact nature and intimate details of the relationship remaining shrouded in vague gossip, hearsay, and innuendo generated by the press, featuring headlines screaming 'Madhuri Dumps Sunjay!' (*Stardust*, June 1993) and 'Sunjay Dutt or Superstardom! Madhuri's Choice' (*Movie*, August 1993). As Majumdar notes, 'the widespread use of innuendo enabled specific screen stories and biographical details to make sense, even without full amplification, because of a generalized discourse of unspecific but salacious knowledge' (2009: 11).

By 1992–3, film journalists acknowledged in their write-ups that Madhuri was rarely tempted into making sensational revelations or controversial remarks – instead she made for 'boring', uncontroversial copy as she herself readily admits:

> Everyone thinks that I am an extremely boring person with a dull lifestyle simply because I don't spout quotable quotes and make exciting copy like the other girls … I don't wish to make exciting copy for anyone. I want people to see my work on screen before labelling me exciting or boring. I am a screen entertainer only. Not an individual entertainer. (*Stardust*, February 1990: 69)

Her 'diplomatic' responses (Biswas 1992) and 'perfectly prioritized public relations' (Kothari 1993) frustrated the prurient Indian press, who accused her of becoming 'mechanical, almost robot-like', since she insisted that all she thought about was acting (Sud 1990: 87).

Thus, Madhuri divulged few personal details, extra-textual information about her being largely restricted to the ordinary and mundane aspects of her professional life. Instead the focus of conversations was often cleverly shifted to spotlight her professionalism and intense work ethic. Her official stance was that there was no time for romance for the 'workaholic' who was also a 'perfectionist,' giving herself 100 per cent to her career while affirming that her 'values, principles [were] intact. They [had] not flown out of the window with stardom' (Divecha 1991). Describing herself as 'sincere and hardworking', acting in six to seven films at once, doing multiple shifts per day (Arora 1989), Madhuri persistently emphasised the labour involved in rigorous rehearsals and constant practice sessions, 'gamely doing retake after retake in the sweltering afternoon sun', to improve and hone her talent.

Unlike many of her contemporaries, she was a thorough professional who fulfilled her commitments. According to Nahta, she 'never troubled her producer and was a producer's and director's delight' (personal communication, 23 June 2013). She had few friends in the industry, and was diplomatic with everyone. She rarely threw tantrums or behaved like a demanding 'diva'; in Nahta's words, she 'never acted pricey' (personal communication, 23 June 2013). Discursively, her publicly controlled private life starkly contrasted with the colourful personal lives of her peers – Sridevi was the 'home wrecker' in a relationship with a married man, Boney Kapoor; Kajol was the wild star kid; Raveena Tandon allegedly had numerous affairs with her co-stars; Dimple Kapadia, having separated from her star husband Rajesh Khanna, was in a relationship with the married Sunny Deol, the son of the legendary actor Dharmendra. While her aforementioned peers represented the New Young Things (NYTs) – 'the Others against whom Dixit represented "traditional values"' (Sircar 2011: 188), she 'played up a non-consumerist lifestyle … . As opposed to the NYT who partied through the night, Dixit was apparently never to be seen at a discotheque' (ibid.: 189). In keeping with her modest lifestyle, she dressed in modest clothing, not even wearing shorts before entering films (Kothari 1995: 29), or make-up at home, always dressing in *salwar-kameez* as opposed to Western clothes … (Sircar 2011: 189). Moreover, she projected an ascetic, asexual self-image, emphatically declaring on numerous occasions that she had never been in love (*Star & Style* 1988b: 68 and Mohamed 1992: 10); never had a boyfriend or been publicly attracted to anyone (*Stardust*, February 1990: 67); never went out on dates ('Madhuri Dixit: One-Up!' 1995: 32); and never read a dirty book or seen a dirty movie (Kothari 1994: 33). She thus personified 'ideal behavior in the domains of kinship and sexuality' (Gandhy and Thomas 1991: 108). Homely and simple, her 'media image re-notated her sexuality as being in consonance with traditional "Indian values" by playing up a middle-class lifestyle' (Sircar 2011: 189).

A fascinating dichotomy can be discerned between her filmic and her private personae. Hers was an asexual off-screen star persona that sharply contrasted with her lusty, erotically charged, sexually provocative on-screen (dance) performances. 'While many argue, that Dixit's performances were far more sensual than her predecessors', Dixit … managed to escape the sex-symbol tag … [her] dance performances [standing] in stark contrast to her conservative public persona' (Mehta 2011: 161). The celebrated Indian painter, M. F. Husain, notorious for his obsessive fandom of Madhuri, notes that she had 'been the essential proper girl. The uninhibited abandon that earned her the "dhak dhak dhamaka" title, she reserved exclusively for on-screen' ('Husain on Madhuri's Marriage!' December 1999: 75).

Sircar insightfully suggests that 'Madhuri Dixit was ideologically constructed as maintaining a distance from the "bad modernity" of the NYTs even while doing "bold" dance numbers as her sexuality was sanctioned by the mediating authority of her traditional upper-caste family' (2011: 189). She willingly submitted herself to the patriarchal control and surveillance of her father (and later her husband). She was indeed, 'prim, proper and practical. Seductive star. Darling daughter' (Biswas 1992). Her homely off-screen image was crucial in offsetting and managing salacious gossip, rumour, and scandal; and negative media coverage which could so easily have tainted her career, ruined her reputation, and undermined her star value and persona (pitfalls that had sealed the fate of many an aspiring Hindi film actress preceding her).

Extra-textually she projected the squeaky clean image of a stereotypical '*Pavitra* Hindu *nari*' (pure Hindu woman) of popular Hindi cinema – thereby conforming to regressive, neo-conservative Hindu nationalist ideologies of denying/controlling/erasing manifestations of female sexuality that had gained populist and political momentum at the time. To avoid the simplistic over-determination of, and dependency on, merely the industrial approach, other contributing factors such as the socio-economic and political context, and technological advancements transforming the 1990s Indian mediascape are examined in Chapter 2 in order to deconstruct the Madhuri Dixit star phenomenon in all its complexities and nuances.

2 A ZEITGEIST ICON

New audio-video technology: The 1980s cassette revolution

The Indian mediascape transformed dramatically between the 1980s and 2000 with the exponential development and growth of the audio and video-cassette industry and the spread of commercial television as a consequence of economic liberalisation, privatisation of media and a gradual turn towards the implementation of neo-liberal policies by the state in the early 1990s. 'The Indian state reduced import tariffs on cassette technology, which in turn increased the affordability and accessibility of cassettes. This flourishing new technology had an impact on both music and film industries' (Bhattacharjya and Mehta 2008: 110). During previous eras, even though *filmi geet* (film songs) had been of tremendous social and cultural importance since their inclusion in *Alam Ara* (*Light of the World*, 1931), India's first 'talkie', in monetary terms they were yet to be fully exploited. 'The advent of cassettes in India paved the way for realizing the commercial potential of film music on an unprecedented scale' (Morcom 2008: 68). First, the music industry was revolutionised by cassettes in terms of 'the size of the music market and the quantum of music sold'. And second, the music industry was decentralised, allowing small producers to enter the market; leading music companies were established, including His Master's Voice aka HMV (now Saregama), Polydor, Venus, Tips, and T-Series, resulting in greater competition; and a variety of music styles were popularised (ibid.: 69). Gulshan Kumar of T-Series, who was killed in 1997, was the single most important figure responsible for the transformation of the music industry. 'While in 1990 only five companies had devoted themselves to the film music business, by 1993 over thirty companies were active in this field' (Bhattacharjya and Mehta 2008: 110). Apart from cassettes, other profitable forms of music and film formats were introduced from 1980s onwards, namely, video, VCD (which continues to enjoy considerable popularity due to its cheap price), DVD, and its pricey cousin, the Blu-Ray. Raminder Kaur and William Mazzarella opine that 'one of the defining features of this period ... was the increasing televisual interpenetration of devotional viewing, political propaganda, and consumer goods advertising', including the unprecedented marketing of film music via the new cassette and video technologies (2009: 17).

Video-cassette technology boom

The television/video boom was the cultural corollary of the liberalisation process. A decisive shift occurred in governmental priorities in the 1980s with the large-scale import of television sets and VCRs. The Asiad games held in Delhi in 1982 inaugurated the arrival of not only colour television but also of video technology in India. The arrival of video ushered in a shift in the perceptual regime of the spectator as media started to be consumed at home. It also led to a liberal regime of tariffs in the electronic industry. Import restrictions were relaxed on video cassettes, video recorders and players (VCRs and VCPs), and television sets, although duties were still high, roughly around 250 per cent.[1] Brands such as Panasonic and Sony distributed video tapes used for recording Hindi films, which led to the mushrooming of video-cassette libraries and parlours, home video tapes, marriage video tapes, and also rampant piracy with bootlegged Hindi film videos flooding the black markets.

One of the biggest all-time blockbusters of India, *HAHK*, starring Madhuri and produced by Rajshri Productions, was infamously described as a three-hour wedding video. Scholars have noted that the massive success of *HAHK* set off a trend for marriage videos on 70mm with Dolby sound. The structure of the film mirrored the events of the North Indian Hindu marriage, the plot stringing together a series of events – 'the ladies sangeet,' the leave-taking, the banquet. The fact that the film replicated the structure of the marriage video had an impact on the marriage-video form as well. Editing and performative techniques in *HAHK* such as the arrangement of scenes, and the ways in which people performed were incorporated in the conceptualisation of marriage videos. In fact, this new technology of amateur, home-made, wedding videography (which had become a media cottage industry from the 80s onwards) is reflexively acknowledged in the film itself when Salman Khan's character, Prem, video-tapes a song and dance number during the marriage of his elder brother. Rajshri Productions' effective marketing strategy instituting a video holdback policy paid rich dividends as it forced audiences to watch the film in theatres. It was also strategically marketed internationally and appealed to conservative, wealthy South Asian diasporas settled in North America, the UK and Australia. Ashish Rajadhyaksha notes that *HAHK* 'was perhaps the first Indian film to recognize and then systematically exploit a marketing opportunity' (2008: 26).

Professional marketing of Hindi film music and song picturisations on commercial television

Television sets saturated the cultural economy of India during the post-1992/3 economic liberalisation era with the exponential growth of the television market and sudden availability of private, cable, and satellite television channels.[2]

> Television ownership grew from 34.9 million in 1992 to 108 million in 2005, while the number of cabled homes shot up from 1.2 million to 60.82 million in the same time span, making India one of the largest cable-connected nations in the world, along with the US (about 70 million) and China (110 million). (Basu 2012: 46)

The monopolies of movie halls and radio were replaced by a plethora of music and movie channels on commercial television which was increasingly the preferred mode of entertainment and recreation for middle-class audiences who had started avoiding decrepit cinema halls. Adrian Athique and Douglas Hill note

> that something that served to mitigate their declining participation in the cinema was the slow growth of television ownership amongst the upper middle classes and the advent of the VCR, which was taken up enthusiastically by these groups throughout the 1980s. (2010: 38)

Madhu Jain observed that this was a decade in which 'the gentile class had retreated to the comfort of television and video,' leaving cinema halls to 'the children of the mean streets' (1990: 46).

'Until the late 1980s and early 1990s when television became widespread, fueled by the new commercial cable and satellite channels, there was no marketing as such of film songs' (Morcom 2008: 70). The spread of commercial television in the early 1990s opened up 'an effective marketing avenue' for the promotion of film songs. As Anna Morcom observes, this period saw 'significant shifts in the dialectic of audience taste and technological possibility and the resulting commercial profitability, popularity, and cultural presence of film songs' (ibid.). Although popular film-song-based programmes such as *Chitrahaar* (*A Garland of Pictures*, 1982–) were telecast on the state-owned channel called Doordarshan, they did not advertise forthcoming films. 'Television advertising started in the late 1980s, and in 1992–3, Doordarshan's monopoly ended with the entry of Star TV, soon followed by other commercial cable channels' (ibid.). In 1994, film-music promotion commenced on television channels such as MTV and Channel [V], proving to be a lucrative and popular advertising platform that saw film-music teasers and trailers played incessantly around the clock, thereby increasing the visibility, reach, and accessibility of song picturisations, and stars featured in these increasingly indispensable music segments. Local cable operators would repeatedly play a montage of popular song sequences. Rajkumar Barjatya of Rajshri Productions, the producer of Madhuri's greatest box-office success, *HAHK*, was the first to recognise that television could be a promotional tool for films, instead of seeing it as a rival medium. 'He started the now standard practice of making trailers, combining clips from the film and the film songs' (ibid.: 71).

Music evolved into 'the single most important marketing device for film' (ibid.: 72), a hit soundtrack often ensuring a film's successful run at the box office. The release of audio cassettes three months before the release of a film only became a norm during this era (ibid.: 66). There is a symbiotic relationship between a film and its songs, one promoting the other. Significantly, several of Madhuri's song picturisations, namely 'Ek Do Teen' (One Two Three), 'Tamma Tamma Loge,' the controversial 'Choli ke Peeche' (Behind the Blouse) and 'Ankhiya Milao' (Making Eyes Meet) were so popular that they were instrumental in the success of the films that featured them – *Tezaab, Thanedaar* (*Jailer*, 1990), *Beta, Khalnayak*, and *Raja* respectively; DVD covers often made prominent mention of the names of the hit songs to promote the sale of these films, and to act as an identifier and nostalgic reminder. The reverse was also true: only after the successful release of *HAHK*, 'one of the most successful Hindi films ever made' (ibid.: 75) did the soundtrack gain traction, selling 'about twelve million cassettes at the time' (ibid.). However, if the film had been a failure, sales figures would have been more modest. Thus, the profitability of film songs changed during this period, and more pertinently, in terms of the dancing star, 'the television era height[ened] the role of spectacle in song picturizations, including stunning locations, glamorous clothes, and elaborate choreography' (ibid.: 79).

It was during the era of cassette and video technology and commercial television that song picturisations, and the stars featured therein, became more emphatically externalised and exteriorised, autonomous, ubiquitous entities, independent of the films themselves, discovering new circuits of marketing and distribution and enjoying markedly extra-diegetic afterlives. While Hindi cinema has been famous for producing 'hit' songs even in previous eras, Ajanta Sircar contends that 'the cassette and television boom precipitated by liberalization in the 1980s not only made music the "dominant" segment of the Bombay film, but created a cultural space for the music sector which is completely autonomous of any film encasing' (2011: 115). Madhava Prasad argues that, in contrast to Hollywood,

> the independently produced Bombay film is marked by the relative autonomy retained by the various elements that flow into the production process. The system of film songs has an autonomous existence … and so do the dialogue and the star image. (1998: 48)

Sangita Gopal and Biswarup Sen note that,

> as an agent of exteriority, ever since the introduction of sound, film songs have enjoyed an existence outside of the films they were written for … . Songs played on radio, cassettes and CDs, and song-dance sequences played on television and on DVDs as well as in clubs and parties constitute a vast extra-textual world which extends far beyond the films where they were originally located. In other words, song-dance established a cultural space which is external to film and autonomous from it. (2008: 151)

Music directors such as Anu Malik, Bappi Lahiri, and A. R. Rahman, and choreographers such as Saroj Khan and Farah Khan began enjoying cult status (Sircar 2011: 115).

The advent of the *filmi* music videos on private cable and satellite television such as Subhash Chandra's Zee Network and Rupert

Murdoch's Star TV enabled the Bollywoodisation of transmedia content – film-based song and dance sequences directed and edited to look like music videos aired continuously as advanced film publicity on numerous film-based music programmes such as *Superhit Muqabla* (1992–4), *Philips Top Ten* (1994–9), *BPL Oye!* (1994–7), *Sa Re Ga Ma* (1995–2005; currently broadcast as *Sa Re Ga Ma Pa Challenge*), *Sansui Antakshari* (1994–2005), and *Meri Awaz Suno* (*Listen to My Voice*, 1995–7). MTV-India 'Bollywoodised' its content by turning to Hindi films and film music for prime-time slots in the late 1990s. 'MTV's music videos became 70 per cent Hindi music videos. Hindi film clips, popular song and dance numbers taken from hit films, made for stupendous, autonomous, self-standing videos, and this in itself effectively Indianized (and localized) MTV' (Punathambekar 2013: 95).

Madhuri's rise to stardom fortuitously coincided with, and benefited from, the film industry's response to the

> emergence of new technologies of mass culture [that] gave rise to a different image of the Star. As opposed to the feudal glamour of Raj Kapoor or Nargis, the media consistently highlighted a certain (urban, upper-class/caste) 'ordinariness' in its portrayal of 1980s' Stars such as Aamir Khan and Madhuri Dixit. (Sircar 2011: 116)

New technology determined the commercial, social, and cultural importance, impact and unprecedented visibility of song picturisations which were largely responsible for Madhuri's popularity and star appeal. I contend that Madhuri was one of India's first major televisual female stars. Sircar, one of the few scholars to have written on Madhuri's stardom, suggests that 'Madhuri Dixit's rise to stardom perhaps best represents the new dominance of music in 1980s' Bombay' (2011: 187). She makes a convincing argument, asserting that Madhuri navigated her route to stardom by capitalising on the increasing importance and visibility of the music segment (via the song and dance spectacle) made possible by the new audio-visual technologies of mass culture. In her words, 'many of the major 1980s' Stars (like Madhuri Dixit) made their claims to Star status primarily through the space opened by the new dominance of music' (Sircar 2011: 115).

Stardom reconfigured during cassette technology and commercial television boom

The relationship of the spectator/fan with the Hindi film star during the cassette era changed irrevocably, engendering new spectatorial practices and relations arising as a result of emergent home-video technology. With the advent of cassette technology, the average Indian spectator/fan was no longer solely dependent on the very public encounter with a star within the confines of a cinema hall. The introduction of video engendered a sense of 'liveness' and led to the emergence of a new form of intimate spectatorship that transformed the experience of familial and conjugal spaces. Television, with its capacity to 'go live,' emphasised its qualities of immediacy and intimacy; bringing stars, stories, song picturisations right into the space of the home; and creating an intimate, private spectatorial experience that is homely, personal, flexible, and portable. For the first time, film stars were inside Indian homes, on the television screen, singing and dancing in domestic spaces, and film fans could conjure them at will at the press of a few buttons, without the travails of travelling to cinema halls.

Thus, in post-1980s India, video technology radically changed the way fans could access, interact, and repeatedly consume their favourite stars within the comfort of their homes or ad hoc communal spaces. As P. K. Mehrotra reminds us, 'for a generation of Indians, the machine [VCR] was their window to the world .... We joined lakhs of Indians in watching Aamir and Madhuri in Dil at home and not the theatre' (2016: 14). The visibility, exposure, and accessibility of stars such as Madhuri changed dramatically due to the emergent audio-visual technology available at home. The ubiquitous presence of stars in popular Indian culture was now possible – ideal conditions for the construction of the first truly televisual superstars able to pervade the public, private, and quotidian lives of ordinary people, capture a nation's imagination, and create a lasting impression and a memorable legacy by appearing in their living rooms. The unprecedented visibility and recall/replay impact factor of stars engendered by the advent of new video technology cannot be overstated and decidedly reconfigured the spectator/star relationship. In fact, it is important to remember that

> the connection between stars and the sensations of everyday life … indicates more of a need to understand the emotional and visceral appeal of stars in the context of globalization rather than simply approaching stardom as a semiotic or discursive phenomenon. (Meeuf and Raphael 2013: 6)

Madhuri's stardom and new avenues of spectatorial consumption of stardom made possible by the availability of emergent home entertainment formats and technology in the form of video cassettes and video-cassette recorders are reflexively acknowledged when Salman Khan's character freeze frames a recording of the song picturisation 'Joote Dedo, Paise Lelo' ('Give Me My Shoes for Money') in *HAHK*. It replicates the way in which a fan would interact with and adore

The advent of new video-cassette technology reflexively acknowledged in *Hum Aapke Hain Kaun…!?* (1994)

his/her star during the new era of video tapes and recorders, pressing the pause button in order to gaze at the frozen image of the 1990s reigning superstar. The ability to replay, rewind, pause, freeze frame song and dance sequences, favourite moments of their stars' performances, their poses, gestures, facial expressions, including the iconic Madhuri smile featured prominently on the poster of *Saajan* and on many DVD cover images of her, facilitated a more personal engagement and involvement with a film star in the privacy of domestic spaces that television would inhabit.

Zeitgeist icon

Apart from the industrial approach adopted in the first chapter, it is imperative to examine Madhuri's rise to stardom within a socio-political context, situating her star phenomenon against the temporal backdrop of a tumultuous decade that saw momentous changes because 'stardom carries a time dimension, which enable us to make a dynamic study of it' (Alberoni 2007: 75). Stars and celebrities 'address and represent (often implicitly) some of the most important political issues of the day …' (Redmond and Holmes 2007: 11). As Francesco Alberoni reminds us, 'stardom appears as a phenomenon appropriate to a certain moment in the development of industrial societies, in which it fulfills certain variable functions which depend on the socio-political configuration of the society' (2007: 75). 'Superstars and cult figures are products of historical moments', Sohini Ghosh suggests,

> emerging from certain socio-historical contexts, they are exceptional individuals whose super-success greatly depends on factors outside of them. Just as Amitabh Bachchan's superstardom could not but emerge in the

Madhuri's signature smile prominently featured on the wall poster of *Saajan* (1991)

1970s, actress Madhuri Dixit's rise to superstardom is inseparable from the hopes and expectations of the 1990s. (2000: 167)

Jyotika Virdi asserts that 'read against and parallel to films, star texts offer a wealth of information about cultural politics, particularly about a particular period [...]' (2003: 137).

Zeitgeist stars attain 'transnational resonance at very particular moments of historical crisis or transition, offering up the ideologies, emotions, and sensations informing subjectivities that are able to manage or assuage the tensions of historical crisis' (Meeuf and Raphael 2013: 6). Madhuri was decidedly both a product and a reflection of her times, mirroring the gendered tensions of globalisation, class, and global modernity mapped onto her star figure. Her rise and reign as commercial Hindi cinema's leading female star encompassed an era of cataclysmic transformations that affected every sphere of life in India – the economy, politics, technology, popular culture, and the media. When she made her debut in 1984, colour TV had only been introduced in India a few years before, but by the time the first phase of her career ended, with her last significant performance, *Devdas* in 2002, there were over 100 television channels. She was a 'zeitgeist icon', able to bridge ideological gaps and tensions by appealing to the ideal of the modern, complete, and discrete individual. Madhuri's body of work squarely situated her in the burgeoning Indian middle-class ethos (Bamzai 2008: 9). Middle-class, aspirational, ambitious India could identify with the arduous struggle of this 'outsider', a status that rendered her achievements remarkable and singular, and with the following sentiments expressed by her: 'I am extremely proud of the fact that I've struggled and what's more survived the struggle … . Because of it, I value my success now much more than I would have valued it if I'd got everything on a silver platter' ('Heartbreaks …' 1989: 27).

According to Deepa Gahlot, Madhuri's success had a lot to do with middle-class women identifying with her:

> She was an outsider in the sense that she did not come from a film family. I think a lot of women felt like she's one of us – added appeal. She wasn't even all that pretty when she came into the industry, spotty skin and all that. Girl-next-door. She did not have to work for a living because she came from a middle class family so it wasn't like she'd starve if she did not make it which gave her a sense of intelligence and values. (personal communication, 26 June 2013)

For Kaveree Bamzai, Madhuri 'represented the ideal urban Indian woman, encapsulating in her uneven body of work, a nation in the midst of enormous flux. To the modern Indian woman, she offered the possibility that she could do it all and have it all' (2008: 28). Inferring from middle-class, female, urban fan responses to the (in)famous 'Choli ke Peeche' song picturisation, Monika Mehta observed that it was 'easy to see why India's middle-class urban women would enjoy' her stunning and sexy dance performances, finding them 'pleasurable because they associate(d) them with sexual agency,' which was lacking in their own lives. 'Their identification with Dixit [was] mediated by the comforting extra-textual knowledge that she too was raised in a middle-class household,' just like them (2011: 183).

Madhuri's stardom and Hindu(tva) nationalism

'Television's rise to prominence within the cultural space of the nation [was] synonymous with a new dominance of the Hindi language [and] the parallel growth of cultural neo-nationalism in India – its most virulent expression being the Hindutva project.'[3] Mega-serials such as *Hum Log* (*We the People*, 1984–5), *Buniyaad* (*Foundation*, 1986–8), *Ramayana* (1987–8) and *Mahabharata* (1988–90) 'all located the essence of the nation within a reconstructed North Indian, patriarchal, Hindu upper-caste social tradition' (Sircar 2011: 112). At a time of dramatic socio-economic and political transformations as cultural colloraries of liberalisation, globalisation, 'invasion' of private satellite and cable television, and the rise of the Hindu Right[4] in early 1990s India, the 'traditional,' sari-clad Madhuri represented to a neo-conservative, middle-class Hindu heartland and the South Asian diaspora reassuring, wholesome images of an Indian womanhood seemingly untouched and unsullied by the 'corrupt' forces of Westernisation. Moreover, her regional identity as a Maharashtrian gave her distinct advantages during this period of Hindu nationalism and the ascendancy of the right-wing political group Shiv Sena, which was rooted in Marathi culture, and headquartered in Bombay (Mumbai), the capital of the state of Maharashtra. Nationalist, parochial forces in the mid-1990s were trying to reclaim Maharashtra as the 'Birthplace of Indian Cinema', and Maharashtrians as the true pioneers of Indian cinema and 'the history of cinema as the sole province of Maharashtrians' (Ganti cited in Kavoori and Punathambekar 2008: 73).

Stars like her perfectly reinforced 'values under threat,' embodying social values that were in crisis in early 1990s India (Dyer 1998: 25). According to Madhuri, *HAHK*, 'spoken of as the biggest hit of the century' ('Madhuri Dixit: One-Up!' 1995: 30), 'revive[d] the family traditions and values which most … [had] almost forgotten today. There was no villain, no blood, no bones breaking, no guns and bullets' (Mohamed 1994: 56). Madhuri felt that in striking a nostalgic tone, 'the film stressed the need for returning to traditional values, and for preserving the joint family system. We have to learn to live together … like we used to in the good old days' ('Madhuri Dixit: One-Up!' 1995: 32).

I contend that her popularity and mass appeal lay in her unique ability to tap into, and allay, the anxieties and moral panics surrounding rampant, indiscriminate Westernisation and the apparent 'corruption' of Indian culture, tradition, and values by the infiltration of 'Western' media. Such wide-ranging political, and social tensions were displaced onto Madhuri's reassuringly traditional, idealised embodiment of femininity, beauty, public propriety, and moral righteousness. As I have examined in the earlier chapter, her personal life was presented in the media as 'boringly' conventional, relatively scandal-free and ascetic – she thus represented to many the quintessential, pure Hindu/Indian womanhood (or *pavitra* Hindu *nari*) who exemplified the regressive gender politics of the Hindu Right, and the general sensibilities of her times.

It is not a mere accident that many of her characters are named after Hindu goddesses (Gauri in *Abodh*, Mohini in *Tezaab*, Ganga in *Khalnayak*, Saraswati in *Beta*, Janaki in *Lajja*) and she rarely played non-Hindu characters. The names signified her character – like the goddess Saraswati, her character resuscitates her husband from near-death (discovering that he is the heir to a large fortune while enduring the life of a poor peasant). As Ganga Gangotri Devi, she is pure, and like Janaki (another name for Sita), her chastity is questioned but in a modern twist, she refuses to take the *agni-pariksha* (trial by fire) in a Ramayana play that she, as a thespian, is enacting. Appropriately, Mohini is the only female avatar of the Hindu god Vishnu. She is portrayed as a femme fatale, an enchantress who maddens lovers, sometimes leading them to their doom.

Initially many of her characters are feisty and outspoken, yet ultimately they conform or capitulate and are eventually disciplined by dominant Hindu patriarchal societal and familial imperatives. As Bamzai points out, 'Madhuri's tremendous talents as an actor were always defined and limited by the roles on offer … . Her screen characters were often trapped in the same old stereotype' (2008: 12–13). Virdi describes *Dil* as 'a sharp satire, a politicized representation of capitalism and patriarchy's imbrication in a new phase of capitalist development in India' (2003: 184). In the film, which incidentally was 'a roaring success at the box office' (ibid.), Madhuri as Madhu is exceptionally feisty. She addresses the eponymous hero Raja (Aamir Khan) thus: 'And my Raja, you better toe the line or else I will sort you out good and proper.' When her father drags her back to their home after he orchestrates hoodlums to beat up her lover, Raja, 'Madhu shows fiery defiance.' When her father threatens to break her legs if she steps outside the house, she boldly retorts: 'Do what you will … . If you break my legs, I'll walk to Raja on my arms, and if you cut my arms off, my body and soul will still desire him' (ibid.: 189). 'Heterosexual romance in *Dil* is radically transgressive. Not only does the couple resist the patriarchal order by breaking social norms, the woman exhibits new aggressiveness in the couple's relationship' in that Madhu initiates their relationship by walking up and publicly kissing Raja in front of her peers and college authorities (ibid.: 191). However, once married, she retreats into the domestic space and slips easily into the traditional gender role of a homemaker, while her husband toils at a construction site, and desists from threatening the status quo.

In similar fashion, Madhuri is the spirited Saraswati in *Beta*, and slaps the villain, a potential rapist; convinces a family not to accept dowry; breaks off her engagement in front of the entire village; and wields a sickle in fights (a recurring motif). She boldly asks the hero (Anil Kapoor) to marry her and offers him 'sindoor' (vermillion). As Madhu in *Raja*, she makes a dramatic entry, reserved for top-billed stars, and is a gutsy prankster and liar who kisses a stranger as part of a bet, and says 'I love you' first, all cultural markers of immodesty and a brash modernity that threatens to upset the patriarchal status quo. Surprisingly forward in such films, she typically initiates romance or expresses her feelings first by approaching the hero and kissing him in public, the media dubbing Madhuri 'the Kiss Miss', which gained her some notoriety. However, her foray into the world of defiance is shortlived, as she is 'quickly reconciled to an establishment figure, she is the good sister to her greedy brothers in *Raja*, or the caring *bahu* (daughter-in-law) to the step-mother-in-law in *Beta*' (Bamzai 2008: 12–13). Madhuri negotiates a fine line between tradition and modernity as exemplified by her diverse character roles of canny, independent girls, bright students, or feisty professionals, and outspoken village belles who suffer little foolishness, especially from leading men (Sen 2014). 'Her career symbolizes a synthesis of conformity and modernity supremely personified in the roller-skating, spirited Nisha of HAHK' (Bamzai 2008: 12), who is one of Madhuri's favourite characters. Although Nisha studies computer science, a signifier of the modern world, she agrees to a marriage with her brother-in-law out of familial pressure and a sense of obligation, thus sacrificing her own desires. As Pooja, 'in DTPH, she is willing to sacrifice her own happiness for her adoptive parents' (ibid.: 13), a gesture with which the star personally identified.

Hindu nationalist iconography and narrative elements

Many of Madhuri's films invoke, or resonate with, the Hindu god and goddess Ram–Sita mythic narrative that ironically overlaps extra-textually with her personal life as she is married to a man named Sriram. In keeping with the Hindu nationalist rhetoric and iconography that permeated many 1990s films, *Khalnayak* can be read as 'a metaphor for – or even a celebration of – the rise of militant Hinduism against the perceived threats from "abroad"' (Thomas 2014: 288). Ballu (Sanjay Dutt), the villain, works for a foreign boss and only his long-lost friend, the police officer Ram (Jackie Shroff), has the authority to punish him. Furthermore, when Ganga's moral and professional reputation is on trial, it at once invokes the trial of the goddess Sita, and the film's dialogue explicitly references the sacred Hindu epic *Ramayana* when Ballu, in a redemptive gesture, comes forth to vouch for her moral virtue and chastity by swearing, on his mother's name, that Ganga is 'pure like Sita' and that 'Ram is Bharat's (India's) true son.' She worships Ram (her love interest) and refers to him as 'my god'; she receives a statue of Ram as a gift from Ballu; and espouses strong Hindu values of faithfulness and loyalty as she rejects the advances of Ballu and stays true to her love, Ram.

In her debut role in *Abodh*, she is a wholesome, innocent Hindu child-bride who remains a virgin throughout the film (much like her projected off-screen persona). Her character is named Gauri, which in Sanskrit means 'white' or 'fair' complexion, after the Hindu goddess and wife of god Shiva. She sings *bhajans* (devotional songs) and offers prayers to Shiva as *tapasya* (penance) when her husband leaves her. Named after two popular Hindu gods, *Ram Lakhan* (1989), Madhuri's first blockbuster is replete with Hindu religious iconography and allusions. Her character is named Radha, after the goddess who is the legendary consort of Lord Krishna. Her love interest is named Ram (Jackie Shroff), and she is seen praying to the god Ram for her Ram. Through editing and the juxtapositioning of shots, there is the suggestion that she is being compared to the goddess Sita, the devoted wife of the god Ram, who is pining for her lover. In this film, Madhuri's first appearance comes in close-ups of her face and her trademark smile in a song picturisation. When the villain, Debbo (Anand Balraj) from America, sees Madhuri's character for the first time, he says 'India is great', as if implying that she is the embodiment of the nation, an exemplary problematic conflation of gender with the nation. In *Thanedaar*, Hindu iconographic allusions include one of the main characters praying to the god Shiva; the temple space being emphasised in its *mise en scène*; the invocation of the mythic story of Abhimanyu's entrapment; and an 'OM' tattoo on the villain Birju's (Sanjay Dutt) arm (reminiscent of the 1975 classic film *Deewar/Wall*) as an identifying mark.

In Lawrence D'Souza's 1991 weepie love triangle *Sajaan*, mythic Hindu references include allusions to the Menaka–Vishwamitra seduction fable and a quote from The Bhagavad Gita, the sacred book of Hindus on the deception of Abhimanyu; and teas are named after the god Ram (*ram pyari*), the tea seller being a devotee of the god Hanuman. Madhuri as Saraswati, the goddess of learning, in *Beta*, is outspoken, gutsy, brave and 'as sacred as the Ganga' who teaches the hero the importance of education. This role gives expression to distinctly feminist undertones of her star persona that are subsequently further developed in off-beat texts such as *Mrityudand, Lajja,* and *Gulaab Gang.* Receiving top billing ahead of Shah Rukh Khan, a testimony of her stature as the leading actress of her time, *Anjaam* (*Consequence,* 1994) is an uncharacteristically violent feminist text about an avengeful woman (in a throwback to the 1980s violent rape–revenge cycle of films), Shivani Chopra (Madhuri), who is seen holding a sickle in her hand, a recurring object motif in many of her films (*Beta, Mrityudand, Gulaab Gang*). Her vengeful avatar and trident in hand invoke in the final death sequences the destructive forces of Hindu mother goddesses. However, although she 'tried to portray a different kind of heroine in *Anjaam,* it was rejected. So [she would] have to', in her words, 'continue being a good girl, a very good girl' ('Madhuri Dixit: One-Up!' 1995: 32). And she certainly did return to her 'good girl' persona with Rajshri Productions' family blockbuster *HAHK,* released the very same year as *Anjaam.* Described by her as 'a sweet film with no maara maari (fighting) just sit back and enjoy the ideal family ... [she] had no idea it would be such a big hit' (Kothari 1995: 26). Madhuri felt that the film was 'a perfect Utopia. ... a world of simple values and guileless human beings' (*Filmfare,* April 1995: 41).

However, many scholars (Bharucha 1995; Juluri 1999; Kazmi 1999; Uberoi 2000; Vitali 2000) have critiqued the utopian Hindu diegetic world, replete with Hindu rituals, rhetoric, allusions, and iconography that espoused 'family values'; the hegemony of the upper-caste, affluent Hindu joint family; the conspicuous consumption, materialism, and hedonism; and the erasure of conflict and dissent. In an audience reception study of *HAHK,* young viewers pointed out how Madhuri's character, Nisha, although a computer programmer by profession, was gradually domesticated by increasing emphasis on her cooking skills (Banaji 2012: 82) so that she would become a suitable wife for Prem (Salman Khan). In keeping with the neo-conservatism of her times, she enthusiastically participates in the numerous Hindu marriage rituals and ceremonies that dominate the diegetic world of *HAHK*. Its 'language environment … neatly formalizes and partitions Urdu', which the stock Muslim character uses in his comical *shairi* (poetry), 'from a highly Sanskritized Hindi that comes to occupy daily life', taking 'over the ceremonial space so completely that even a group photograph is called "samyukh chitra"'. Neo-conservative slogans such as 'I love my family' adorn the young hero Prem's room (Basu 2012: 82). Hindu gods are invested with narrative agency as divine intervention in the form of Tuffy, the dog touched by Lord Krishna, alerts the man Nisha is being forced to marry. In a much later film, Yash Chopra's romantic triangle *DTPH*, a box-office success produced by Yash Raj films, and starring the superstar Shah Rukh Khan, divine intervention in the form of a crystal Ganesha is seen to clarify matters when Madhuri, as the dreamy Pooja, must decide between duty and passion, much like *HAHK*'s Nisha.

Fareed Kazmi notes, 'HAHK ends up as regressive and archaic … [it] sanctifies tradition as opposed to the modern and re-entrenches a social system that is feudalistic, patriarchal and rigidly hierarchical' (1998: 188–9). She attributed such regressive gender politics to Hindu nationalist parties such as the Vishwa Hindu Parishad (VHP) and the Bharatiya Janata Party (BJP) 'and the emergence of the political concept of the Sangh Parivar' (1998: 191). Rustom Bharucha discerns 'a deep internalisation of the Hindu Right in popular and mass culture' (1995: 804) without which this film could not have been produced, while Valentina Vitali asserts that the film contributed to 'the discourse of Hinduisation' also deployed by the BJP (2000). '[T]he conspicuous materialism of *HAHK* is reconciled with an incipient Hindutva in what sociologist Dipankar Gupta calls "the rise of predatory patriotism" in which Congress' New Economic Policy led to the dismantling of Nehruvian secularism' (cited in Bamzai 2008: 15). Raminder Kaur and William Mazzarella observe how

> the stunning expansion of commercial entertainment-based television … brought together, in a volatile compact around the affect-intensive television image, a range of new middle-class aspirations, the blandishments of consumerism, and a mass acceptance of an overtly and frequently aggressive religious nationalism (2009: 17)

all of which were exemplified by the diegesis and audience reception of *HAHK*.

Madhuri is the low-caste village belle, Kajri, in Rajiv Kapoor's film *Prem Granth* (*Book of Love*, 1996) that begins with 'Hail Ram' slogans during its pre-credit sequence; deploys the iconography of the Hindu village fair; and once again foregrounds outdoor and residential temple spaces in its *mise en scène*. Madhuri's character is named Gauri (yet again) in *Koyla* (*Coal*, 1997), and notably makes her first appearance at a temple to the accompanying religious chants of 'OM' by a priest. In Rajkumar Santoshi's *Pukar* (*Call*, 2000), 'Madhuri embodies a more aggressive post-Kargil Hindu nationalism' (Bamzai 2008: 16). Two years later, in Santoshi's *Lajja*, a feminist film of the actress's late career showcasing her performative skills, she is the outspoken and defiant Janki (significantly, another name for Sita), who is asked to perform a character test by agreeing to her husband's demand of aborting their child since he is unsure whether the child is his, a test that has a parallel with the god Ram's behaviour towards his wife Sita, and casts aspersions on her moral character. However, in a surprising twist to the epic Hindu tale of Ramayana, Janki refuses to perform the *agni-pariksha* (trial by fire). It is a brave and unconventional role of an abandoned woman deserted by her husband, assaulted in public, and stomped on by an angry mob. Indeed, 'for an actress topping the A-list, Dixit frequently avoided predictability, taking chances with her scripts, directors, and co-stars' (Sen 2014) in a concerted effort to avoid typecasting, by accepting a diverse range of roles especially during the latter years of the first phase of her career.

Consolidating her stardom, Madhuri expanded her performance range by starring in two critically acclaimed feminist texts, Jha's *Mrityudand* and Santoshi's *Lajja*, proving to her critics that she was more than just a dancer who could also act. Even a cursory glance at both films' official posters reveals the unconventional, off-beat woman-centric focus. Historically, Hindi cinema posters feature and foreground male stars, with actresses/female stars receiving scant attention and, if featured at all, they are usually depicted in titillating poses and costumes of sex objects (as on the *Khalnayak* poster). Instead, the bilingual *Mrityudand* poster centres Madhuri's deglamourised, gun-toting figure, and textually the Hindi header reads 'Centuries of Silence – the Voice of Woman ...'; while the *Lajja* poster in Hindi is striking for the complete absence of male characters; four headshots of only female characters are featured as celebration of woman power. Denied roles of substance for many years, Madhuri snatched whatever opportunities came her way, most spectacularly *Mrityudand*, in which she plays Ketki, a gutsy rural woman battling gender oppression in feudal Bihar. Neither does she allow her husband to cross the line: 'You are my husband. Don't try to act like my lord and master.' She initiates revolt against the corrupt contractors who have terrorised her family and confronts one of them in a chilling scene when they enter her bedroom. With a sickle held aloft like the goddess Kali, a powerfully visceral motif used in *Beta* and later in *Gulaab Gang*, she says, 'You have not only killed my husband but also the honour of women. I won't spare you.'

Despite her acting talent, performance range, and beauty, Madhuri is best remembered for her extraordinary dancing talent that was considered to be, for lack of a better phrase, a 'game changer' in Hindi cinema. As Usha Iyer observes, Madhuri was acclaimed 'for introducing a new sensuality to film dance. She was seen as a harbinger of novel, trademark moves and as the definitive female dancing star of the period, whose song-and-dance numbers

Mrityudand (1997) and *Lajja* (2001) posters reflecting the rare dominance of female characters

were often bigger draws than the films themselves' (2015: 310). Describing boisterous, participatory audiences' 'Madhuri mania' in cinema halls, Anupama Chopra writes:

> Wearing a backless embroidered orange choli, she [Madhuri] grinds and thrusts in her trademark 'Dhak Dhak' style. The whistles grow deafening when she stares into the camera, looks at every man in the dark, and promises him her heart – and much more. In one Bangalore theatre, the police were kept on standby in case the crowds went beserk. (2011: 39)

3 THE DANCING STAR

How and why were song and dance sequences important in establishing Madhuri as a dancing star? What role did they play in the construction of her star persona and what is her contribution to Hindi film dance? What about her distinctive performance style[1] (especially her facial expressions and body language) that made her the leading dancing star of her generation? These are some of the questions that are explored in this chapter, which also examines questions of genre, star vehicles, costuming; and how expressive and narrative devices were effectively deployed to construct an endearing, innocent-yet-sensual star persona.

Dancing to stardom: Genre and star vehicles

Late 1980s popular Hindi cinema offered limited, stereotypical, one-dimensional roles for women – dancing, and the song sequence, were the only aspects of popular, commercial cinema through which an actress could make a lasting visual impact, showcase her talent, and even outshine male co-stars. During this period, there were considerable industrial limitations and narrative constraints for actresses to overcome. 'In a decade devoted to action and vendetta of the bloodlust kind, the heroine was reduced to the hero's side-kick. A pretty and sexy backdrop to the hero's heroics' (Jain 1990). They were primarily meant to be attractive, decorative showpieces, veritable eye-candies who would mouth a few lines of clichéd dialogue, and look pretty. 'The director took a back seat while dance and fight directors grabbed the baton. Fight directors began to choreograph the increasing number of rape scenes. Films began to have multiple villains to take on the multiple heroes and heroines' (ibid.). Distributors demanded a minimum number of fight and rape scenes while the influence of directors' consumption of videos of B-grade foreign films resulted in a spate of cheap imitative remakes.

Historically, dance had been an integral part of commercial Hindi cinema, offering a unique performative space for actresses to showcase their talents and navigate a path to stardom. However, 'it was only a selected group of heroines who really danced, such as Vyjayanthimala, Madhubala, and Meena Kumari, and only in certain roles where the dance was clearly chaste, or, for example, in the role of a courtesan' in pre-1970s eras. Thereafter, as Anna Morcom suggests, 'it gradually became not just the norm, but essential, for the heroine to be a good dancer and to be featured in several dances in the film that would present her erotically' (Morcom 2011: 169), and extensive sequences showcased an expanding repertoire of audacious dance moves from such stars as Hema Malini, Sridevi, and Madhuri Dixit.

The 1980s 'masala' film, 'a culinary term that seeks to define a medley of narrative strands in popular cinema' (Gopalan 2002: 18), was a multi-generic 'formula' for box-office success that included action, romance, comedy, and melodrama, creating opportunities for multiple spectacles of various types – songs, fights, dances, comedy, and foreign locations – meant to ensure audiences received their money's worth (*paisa vasool*). For Madhava Prasad, this 'super genre' asserted 'its dominance through narrative strategies of annexations' whenever new subgenres emerged … 'Instead of discrete genres, a megalomaniac genre cannibalises the formation of sub-genres' (Gopalan 2002: 18). 'An all-in-one portmanteau' (Bhatia 2013: 70), the masala spectacles, especially in the form of song and dance sequences, were often presented as a series of set pieces, episodic in nature, that created repeat and recall value.

This was also the era of 'multi-starrers' or films featuring multiple stars, usually male, who would ensure box-office revenue on release by pulling in their established fan base, in an attempt to maximise profits and minimise risks. Moreover, it was an era defined by mass-appeal movies intended for the so-called front-benchers (the cheapest seats in movie halls), as 'good families' had retreated to their homes to watch movies and Pakistani serials on their VCRs. Madhuri's biggest hits 'were made by filmmakers who catered to this mass culture, including N. Chandra and Indra Kumar (a Gujarati actor-turned-director, who made the enormously successful *Dil*, *Raja*, and *Beta* in partnership with his East African friend, producer Ashok Thakeria), and Subhash Ghai …' (Bamzai 2008: 22).

Madhuri successfully prised open and exploited the subversive potential and the permissive, seductive space of song sequences that attracted mass audiences and front-benchers, thereby escaping the narrative confines of scripted gender stereotypes in expressing overt female sexuality, desire, and agency through erotic dances and provocative costuming. These spaces, created for and by her, were the fissures through which moments of excess, of visual pleasure, could be articulated, allowing her to transcend the limitations of poorly written and uninspiring characterisations, and display her sensual dancing skills, her female form, poise, grace, her *adda* (style), and her ability to tease the hero. Thus, the song and dance sequence was a major star vehicle for Madhuri in which she usually danced alone, or with another female star, while the hero/male star remained an admiring onlooker and bystander, outperformed by her extraordinary dancing talent through 'numerous solo "highlights" – Manmohan Desai's phrase for autonomous vignettes with little relation to plot and designed mainly to showcase the star's versatility' (Rajadhyaksha and Willemen 1999: 530). Undoubtedly, dance sequences, typically dominated by actresses, were excellent opportunities for upstaging male stars and subverting conventional male-oriented narratives and characters.

Richard Dyer defines the star vehicle as providing 'a character of the type associated with the star ...; a situation, setting or generic context associated with the star ...; or opportunities for the star to do her/his own thing ...' (1998: 62). Promotional conduits for stars, 'the star vehicle combines two methods of product differentiation: the personal monopoly of a star's image, and the familiar conventions that establish generic expectations' (McDonald 2000: 93). Neepa Majumdar discusses song sequences as potent star vehicles that, through music, 'performance techniques', and changes in costume and setting, 'represent the most idealized aspects of star presence' (2009: 175). For Dyer, the star vehicle provides

> continuities of iconography (i.e. how they are dressed, made-up and coifed, performance mannerisms, the settings with which they are associated and so on), visual style (e.g. how they are lit, photographed, placed within the frame) and structure (e.g. their role in the plot, their function in the film's symbolic pattern).

It is the continuities of iconography, style, and structure across a star's body of work that lead Dyer to compare star vehicles to genres in that they create a set of conventions and predictable audience expectations akin to generic categories (McDonald 2000: 95). Thus, the Madhuri film became synonymous with scintillating song and dance sequences, the omission of which would prove an enormous disappointment to expectant, cine-literate Hindi film audiences wanting their *paisa vasool* (money's worth). Playing to her strength as star vehicles are meant to facilitate, Madhuri recalls producers and directors adding 'songs-and-dance numbers to her films,' thereby allowing her, in Dyer's words, 'to do her own thing' (Walavalkar 1991: 14). Permissive spectacles, these sequences transformed the (good) girl-next-door image into an embodiment of explicit sensuality. Within the frame, she became a vortex of sexual energy; a singularly charismatic presence, creating a lasting sensorial impression.

'I love dancing. I have a lot of rhythm in my body, which I now let go wild':[2] Performance style and the star body

From 1980s onwards, film dance became critical in the construction of female stardom. Usha Iyer contends that, as

> the inaugurator of a new regime of dancing that had long-ranging implications for the construction of female stardom, Dixit functions as a critical figure in investigating changes in the Hindi film's aesthetic, narrative, and industry configurations since the late 1980s. (2015: 131–2)

She consistently overshadowed her male co-star, stole the show from him, and asserted her own stardom. Madhuri as a dancing spectacle maximised screen time and space through song and dance segments that created a recall effect, and a lasting visceral impact generating 'repeat value'. While the spotlight was firmly on her, the hero was reduced to spectating at the edge of the frame or feebly matching her dance moves only to be eventually eclipsed by her technical mastery. The focal point of the dance spectacle, Madhuri diverted and distracted spectatorial attention away from the hero. The cynosure of all eyes, she would dominate screen space and time, and often did not share the frame with the hero when she danced. In the song picturisations 'Choli ke Peeche Kya Hai,' 'Dhak, Dhak,' and *DTPH*'s 'Dance of Envy,' Madhuri staged her dance performances for the pleasure of the diegetic heroes (played by Sanjay Dutt, Anil Kapoor, and Shah Rukh Khan respectively) and the spectator, who shared the hero's lustful 'male gaze'. Usually performed in front of an enthralled diegetic audience, her dances were presented, through formal techniques, as staged set pieces with a tableau-style frontal address, Madhuri often looking directly at the camera/spectator, thus breaking the fourth wall.

The dynamic star body, undeniably centred, dominated the proscenium-like performance space. Dance routines accentuated the centrality of the desired/desiring dancing star body; the sheer physicality and corporeal presence of the dancer, meticulously choreographed and captured by the cinematographer from various shot scales and flattering angles, eliciting visceral, primal, scopophiliac pleasure of the kind deeply appreciated by M. F. Husain. According to him, she had

> a great face and body rhythm which reminded him of Greta Garbo, Marilyn Monroe and Meryl Streep. She move[d] a little finger and her entire body seem[ed] to be alive as if there was an electric current running through her. (Shahani 1995: 34)

Iyer argues that 'this immanence of the star body, of body as body rather than as a vehicle for a diegetic character, makes dance and action sequences central devices in constructing the iconicity of certain star bodies' (2015: 134). The spectacularly mounted Madhuri dance routines are 'structured around a display of one or more dancing bodies, highlighting the experiential rather than the narrational pleasures of the text' (ibid.: 135).

Madhuri's stardom was constructed around her dance performances in song picturisations, in effect star vehicles, meticulously choreographed by Saroj Khan, who taught her protégée, the best dancer that she had ever worked with (Ghosh 2000), not just dance moves and skills, but also *abhinaya* or 'the art of expression', a concept in classical Indian dance and drama derived from the ancient text *Natya Shastra*. Khan was 'a central figure in the redefinition of dance moves in the late 1980s and the 1990s, introducing an earthy and bawdy movement vocabulary dominated by the heaving of the chest, pelvic thrusts, and exaggerated swaying of the hips' (Iyer 2015: 137). The ultimate *filmi* dance guru, whose imaginative dance moves and mastery over various dance traditions (folk, street, classical, and cabaret) had powered many star careers, Khan was instrumental in expanding the repertoire of a heroine's hitherto modest and restrictive dance 'movement vocabulary,' (to quote Iyer), appropriating the raunchy moves and costuming of vamps, as the lines between heroine/vamp blurred during the 1990s. Madhuri developed a distinctive array of body movements (head, hand, limb, upper torso, back), gestures, and postures; learned to time the appearance of her all-important radiant smile while dancing, and to 'dance with her face', employing a range of facial expressions (comic, seductive, naughty, innocent) to facilitate storytelling through the art of *abhinaya*.[3]

Under Khan's strict and able tutelage, Madhuri honed her craft during her difficult transformative years. Specifically, she learnt how to enter and exit from a frame, which could look sloppy, especially in song-and-dance sequences, acknowledging that it was while working with Khan in *Uttar Dakshin* that she 'learnt how to literally glide into a frame', with an element of 'grace' and 'a certain smoothness' (Mohamed 1997: 62). Quite significantly, Madhuri says she

> realized that dance in films was very different from that on stage. On stage you have more freedom to move around. For a film, you have to keep in mind the markings and also look into the camera at the same time. (Farook 2011)

Khan, a reputed perfectionist, taskmaster, and disciplinarian, assisted her favourite star pupil (*shishya*) to master difficult dance steps and complex moves through rigorous and repeated rehearsals, and numerous retakes.[4] In 1988, she recalls how Madhuri had

> improved tremendously from her *Uttar Dakshin* days where she used to be very stiff. In *Tezaab*, she laboured a lot. Every day she used to come and rehearse for two hours, at times just to polish her steps. Now she picks up what I tell her very fast. (Jagirdhar-Saxena 1989)

Directing Madhuri in his debut film *Gulaab Gang*, Soumik Sen observes the star's uncanny knack of picking up new and complex dance steps within seconds, and her desire to push herself to perfect dance movements in retake after retake (personal communication, June 2013).

Evidently, Khan played a pivotal role in sharpening Madhuri's technical skills, impeccable timing, and innate sense of rhythm, which tapped into the star's natural flair for, and enjoyment of, dance. Iyer applies and extends Majumdar's key conceptualisation of the 'dual star text' produced by the combination of the on-screen actress's body and the off-screen voice of the playback singer to the potent combination of the behind-the-scenes master choreographer and the on-screen female dancing body. As she insightfully suggests, 'given the pervasive role of Khan's choreography in the construction of the Dixit star text, one could conceive of a dual star text in this instance, combining the choreographic prowess of Khan with the performance skills of Dixit' (Iyer 2015: 137).

Madhuri's iconic dance performances began with *Tezaab*'s 'Ek Do Teen', which turned her into an overnight sensation. In fact, to quote *Star & Style*, 'Madhuri put in so much of verve, life, oomph into her "Tezaab" number that a sexy Madhuri dance number [became] mandatory in every film she signed subsequently' ('How Success Has Changed Madhuri Dixit' 1991: 17). 'Ek Do Teen' was seen to mark such a significant shift in Hindi film dance choreography that the popular Filmfare Awards instituted an award for best choreography in 1989 which was presented to Saroj Khan, the choreographer of this sequence (Iyer 2015: 137). A variation on the Madhuri-dominated song and dance sequence was the dance-off (dubbed as a *jugalbandi* or a competitive duet by the popular film press), in which she would be pitted against a rival female star she would typically outshine such as the younger Aishwarya Rai in the 'Dola Re Dola' song picturisation from *Devdas* and Karisma Kapoor in the 'Dance of Envy' song sequence from *DTPH*.[5] One notable exception was 'Kay Sera... Sera...' (Whatever Will Be Will Be) from *Pukar* in which she paired with South Indian dance sensation, Prabhu Deva, dubbed

India's Michael Jackson. Here was a meeting of two dancing icons, matching each other step for step, and showcasing their extraordinary dancing skills. 'The choreography of the song also by Deva ushers in an androgynous and plastic style that has so far not been performed by any woman in Bombay' (ibid.). Madhuri, at the time written off due to her age and recent marriage, reminded audiences why she was still considered the best female dancer in the industry.

Why is Madhuri a great screen dancer?

This section intends to dispel misconceptions, and repudiate the popular assumption, that Madhuri was 'born' a naturally gifted, on-screen dancing star. Populist narratives of stardom display a predilection for obfuscating the seminal trope of star labour and character attributes inherent in the achievement of sustained artistic success and fame. Instead, I hope to accentuate her awkward years in which she struggled to learn the art of dancing for the camera, underscoring the differences between classical dance performed live on stage and *filmi* dance that is dictated by the camera, along with the challenges she overcame in mastering complex dance moves that appeared seemingly effortless on screen. I also draw on a range of informed opinions from dance maestros and artists that validate Madhuri's iconic status as an incomparable Hindi film dancer. Contrary to popular belief, Madhuri was aggressively promoted as a potential dancing star by producers and directors long before her breakthrough performance in *Tezaab*, as evident from full-page trade-paper advertisements:

Madhuri with your electrifying Performance in UTTAR DAKSHIN (sic) You've sent shockwaves in the industry & with your dances you've danced your way into the audience's hearts! Greater Glories Await you in Tezaab. – Dinesh Gandhi, N. Chandra (*Film Information*, 21 November 1987)

During the early years of struggle, a period marked by successive box-office failures, Madhuri was pilloried in the media for her dancing. *Star & Style* proclaimed: 'As an actress she was no great shakes, but as a dancer too she was bad' ('How Success Has Changed Madhuri Dixit' 1991: 17), referring to her as 'the stiff "Uttar Dakshin" girl' (ibid.). She even criticised herself retrospectively, describing her dancing in *Uttar Dakshin* as 'clumsy' and 'stilted' while explaining the difficulties she faced in adjusting, emphasising the difference between on-screen dancing and dancing on stage, and how her years of training in classical dance (*kathak*) failed to help with '*filmi* dancing', which is dictated by the camera. She admitted she 'was awfully clumsy in that film, though having been a classical dancer at a young age, [she'd] had a number of stage performances at school to [her] credit!'

> I think the main reason for my stilted movements was the restriction that was imposed upon me. I was used to dancing on the whole big stage free for movement, but dancing before the camera was a different thing. The markings on the ground monitored my movements. The result was that I was more bothered about following the markings than about my dancing. It is only now after all these years – six to be exact – that I have learnt to relax in front of the camera. That must be the reason for my successful 'Ek Do Teen'. … (ibid.: 17).

In the same year, in yet another candid interview, this time with the leading trade paper, *Screen*, Madhuri revealed that she 'found dancing in films most difficult to do'. She 'was used to classical dance – Kathak and all classical dance has a certain discipline. *Filmi* dancing is however camera dictated. One leg flung here, an arm waving there – it's all camera' (Walavalkar 1991: 14). She recalled gradually picking up on how easy it was to exceed the range of the camera with one extra step, realising in time that 'to dance well in films [was] an art in itself' (ibid.) She felt it was imperative to possess 'an inherent sense of rhythm more than anything else. A sense of grace that is inborn. A fluidity of movements that is natural and the ability to look comfortable doing ridiculously intricate steps' in odd situations and locations 'dressed in outlandish costumes. No training in classical dance can give you that' (ibid.).

In interviews for such popular film magazines as *Showtime*, she refers to specific dance routines and intricate steps that, although seemingly effortless, were difficult to execute, and required considerable skill and concerted effort to master. She divulges that the legendary classical dance maestro, Birju Maharaj, told her that he would only teach her if she showed him 'how she did those backwards steps in *Ek, do, teen*!' In her words,

> that movement looks easy but it's very difficult to do … the dance that really foxed me was a step in *Choli ke peechey* where, in that line *Resham ka lehnga mera*, I had to stand on one foot while turning the other foot, and turn the hands also, shake one leg like that, shake one hand like that and there was a *kamar* (hip) movement too. That really stumped me … but I managed after rehearsals. ('Madhuri's Personal Notes on Mr Right' 1993: 23)

Another dance routine for which she rehearsed intensely, needing forty takes to perfect, was Bappi Lahiri's disco-influenced, foot-tapping number 'Tamma Tamma' from the box-office dud *Thanedaar*. At the end of the number they had to throw their hats onto their own feet, which was really tricky since 'sometimes that hat would just roll off or it wouldn't land on the foot!' (ibid.).

Celebrated painters, dance gurus, photographers, and film critics, at various stages of Madhuri's impressive career, have pointed out reasons why she is arguably the best dancer in the history of popular Hindi cinema. 'The main thing about Madhuri', according to Husain, was 'the unity in her body and posture. She reacts intuitively to a given situation, all her nerves and muscles seems to act spontaneously. She's animated, she's in complete technical control.' He observed that in the song from *HAHK*, 'Didi Tera Devar Deewana' (Sister, Your Brother-in-Law Is Crazy), 'where she juts out her torso … where she's pretending

Difficult dance movements in 'Tamma Tamma' (*Thanedaar*, 1990) and 'Choli Ke Peechey' (*Khalnayak*, 1993) song picturisations

to be pregnant ... is marvelous. If it was any other actress, it would have looked vulgar' (Shahani 1995: 38). For him, while other actresses projected vulgarity, there was 'a spiritual quality about Madhuri's body' (Pammi 1999a: 51). Well-known dancer-choreographer, Shiamak Davar expressed a popular sentiment that I frequently heard during my fieldwork – like many others in the industry, he 'would give anything to dance with Madhuri on screen'. Rating her after Helen, he felt that she was 'simply phenomenal, she moves so well and her expressions are just fabulous ... . Like Rekha, Madhuri is a legend in her own right. You can't erase her from your mind' (Karmalkar 1998: 13). *Movie* gushed about how Madhuri could 'move as fast as the beat of the music and whether it's Birju Maharaj or Gopi Krishan, noted dance masters have oohed and aahed (sic) over Madhuri's terpsichorean technique'; 52 per cent of voters in a movie poll declaring 'Madhuri's moves as sheer poetry in motion' ('Movie Poll', March 1998: 72). Noted celebrity photographer Gautam Rajadhyaksha was struck by how photogenic the dancing diva was, stating that 'Madhuri and Manisha Koirala were two actresses with the least bad angles' (Masand 1997: 16). Reviews, such as the following, took note of the importance of the dance choreographer to a film's success. In the *Screen* review of *DTPH*, film critic and author Maithili Rao mentioned 'Madhuri dancing like an *apsara* to Shah Rukh Khan's heart-throbbing drums', observing that 'the key to the stylistic success of this film [lay] in the choreography. Choreography not only of the dances which are superb ensemble pieces and mainstream Hindi cinema's first "balletic modern dance" but that of pacing the film itself ...' (Rao 1997: 10).

Sanjay Leela Bhansali's version of *Devdas*, based on the novel by the famed Bengali author Sarat Chandra Chatterjee, and adapted for film at least five times, featured nine song picturisations emphasising dance more than any of its predecessors, making it the ideal star vehicle for Madhuri. The most prominent dance is 'Dola Re Dola', a shared public performance by Paro (Aishwarya Rai), Devdas's unrequited love, and Chandramukhi (Madhuri), the courtesan in love with Devdas, thus representative of the typical 1990s love triangle. The film's publicity, press reviews, and theatrical trailers revolved around the spectacular 'dance-off' between the two leading actresses, both known for their classical dance training; Rai was played up by the media as a rival and heir to the position of top female star enjoyed by Madhuri for much of the 90s decade in typical sensationalist fashion: 'Such is the climate of shifting tides at the box-office ... yesterday Sridevi, today Madhuri, tomorrow Aishwarya [...]' ('Madhuri-Ash Clash! Sanjay's Revenge?' 2002: 54).

Chandramukhi's dances, choreographed by Pandit Birju Maharaj, make this a perfect exemplar of a star vehicle created

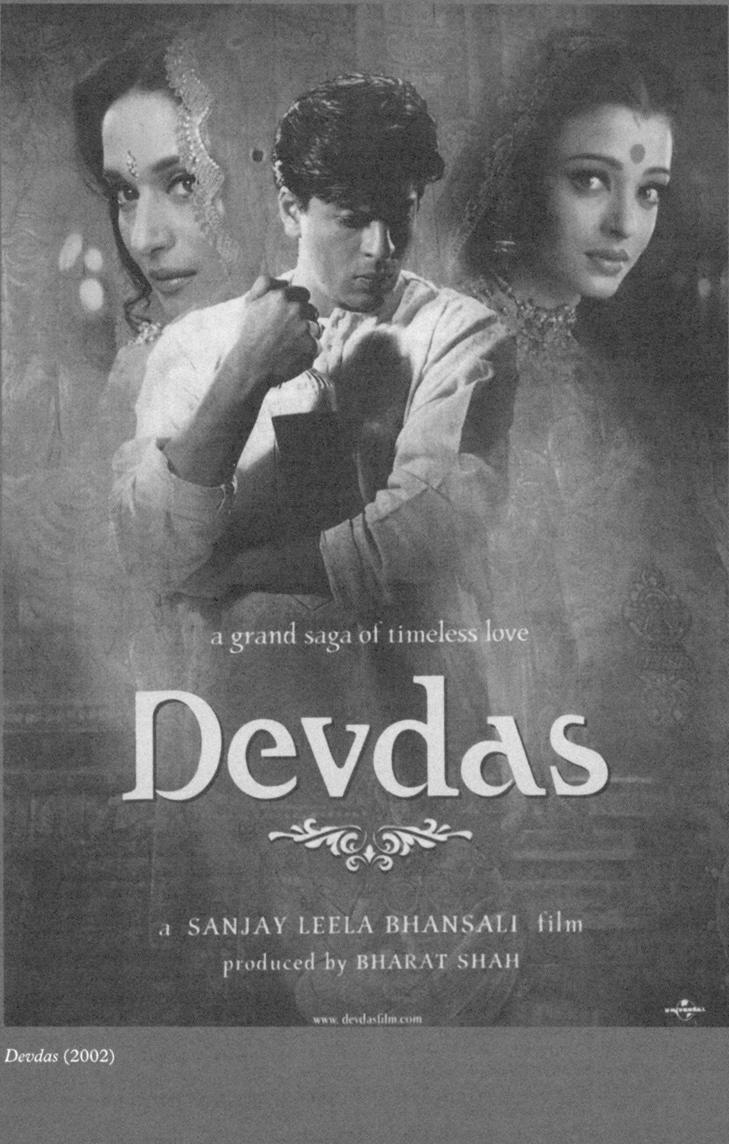
a grand saga of timeless love
Devdas
a SANJAY LEELA BHANSALI film
produced by BHARAT SHAH
www.devdasfilm.com

Devdas (2002)

to showcase Madhuri's dancing skills. As Sangita Shresthova points out,

> Dixit's technical mastery of complex rhythms are accented (sic) through rhythmically coordinated camera cuts; her ability to emote through facial expression and gesture is emphasized through close-ups ... This attention to her skills marks Dixit's rendition of Chandramukhi different from previous representations.

Her virtuosity even surpassed that ofVyjayanthimala Bali, considered a dancing star in her heyday (Shresthova 2008: 253). For Husain, who decided to immortalise her role on canvas and take his exhibition of Madhuri as Chandramukhi to different parts of India, 'Madhuri [was] the eternal Chandramukhi' ('Madhuri-Ash Clash! Sanjay's Revenge?' 2002: 54). According to *Variety* film critic, Derek Elley,

> The chemistry in this scene between the two actresses eclipses anything thus far. And it sets the scene for the next musical number, a joyful, highly rhythmic dance led by the two femmes, which is an instant, hair-raising Bollywood classic. (2002: 25)

Madhuri, describing their dance duet as 'more camaraderie than competition,' felt both of them were 'dancing in ecstasy' (Pradhan 2002: 52). She also lavished praise on her co-dancer's skills, commenting that Rai was a great dance companion, 'quick on the uptake,' and 'very graceful' (ibid.).

Sensuous yet not vulgar: Expressive and textual devices

Madhuri's star text is defined by her audaciously provocative dance routines, and yet intriguingly, her wholesome, good girl image endures. How was this achievable? I believe that this question holds the key to fathoming her continuing popularity, unsullied reputation, and mass appeal. Similar to Marilyn Monroe, who embodied both innocence and sensuality at the same time, Madhuri had the remarkable ability to reconcile the on-screen glamorous, seductive aspects of her star image with the wholesome, traditional, 'good girl' off-screen persona that was rooted in her middle-class upbringing and Maharashtrian background, as examined in Chapter 1.

Madhuri's innocent, radiantly smiling face coupled with a voluptuous sensuality evokes Dyer's examination of Monroe's contradictory stardom that combined, at once, elements of sexuality and innocence (1987), as she effortlessly straddled the gendered stereotypes and fractured subjectivities of 'virgin' and 'whore' (Meeuf and Raphael 2013: 4). Madhuri explains how 'instead of making the dance cheap by tossing my face and body aggressively, [she] deliberately brought innocence, laughter and sweetness into [her] eyes and face so that people would notice [her] facial expression more than [her] body' (Bamzai 2008: 18). Her most ardent fan, Husain certainly noticed her eyes and facial expressions. Watching *HAHK* for a staggering sixty-seven times 'to celebrate the mystique of Madhuri', he was most struck by

> the nuances, the expressions which flicker on her face. The closing and opening of eyes [were] like the apertures of a camera ... I am fascinated by her movements and expressions. She is the route towards a higher feeling of creativity. (Shahani 1995: 34)

The dancing diva's contrasting body/face figuration is fascinating. Reputed for her iconic sensual dances, she retained 'a surprising level of innocence, her oomph always leavened by her disarming smile' (Bamzai 2008: 17). Radiantly smiling while striking provocative dancing poses, one can discern a dichotomy between the star face and body. Half-closed, shy eyes, innocent (and occasionally comic) facial expressions, and a charmingly crooked smile, reminiscent of Madhubala, helped offset her raunchy body movements and gestures. Expressive of naïve youthfulness, trade expert Komal Nahta

Madhuri's breakthrough song and dance sequence 'Ek Do Teen' in *Tezaab* (1988)

points out that the 'purity of her face' may have been responsible for reconciling the tensions underlying the contrasting face/body juxtaposition (personal communication, June 2013).

In an attempt to decipher 'Madhuri Magic', Anupama Chopra wrote in an *India Today* review:

> So what is the Madhuri phenomenon all about? It's about dancing, for one. No other actress can match her suggestive, come-hither mobility. In the profusion of bare midriffs and wiggling hips, her sexuality stands apart, *marked by an apparent innocence. Her expressive eyes retain a childlike look even as the breasts heave and the pelvis thrusts*. Her slim body lends grace to the most blatant and suggestive choreography. (2011: 40; emphasis added by author)

According to Deepa Gahlot, she escaped being labelled vulgar or obscene because 'her background had something to do with it. Everyone knew she came from a middle-class background … I think her image of a regular, nice girl stood her throughout' (personal communication, 26 June 2013). Her co-star, Anil Kapoor felt she had 'amazing grace. Even her *Dhak dhak* dance in *Beta* was sensuous … there was no vulgarity' (Nilesh 1996: 30). Madhuri's vocal attributes and singing voice are often ignored in an appraisal of her stardom. She had a non-vampy, innocent, youthful speaking voice, and a singing voice, usually dubbed by the playback singer Anuradha Paudwal, who herself had a 'clean' and wholesome reputation in the film-music industry, singing romantic songs and *bhajans* (devotional songs). Incidentally, according to Nahta, Madhuri could modulate her voice very well, and was an exceptionally good dubbing artiste.

'The heroine can now make a pass': Exonerating textual devices

Prasad analyses Hindi film dances as sites of temporary permission, providing glimpses of the otherwise hidden, prohibited, private sphere; creating spaces for the transient relaxation of moral and sexual codes of behaviour that could even represent transgressive expressive realms (1998).[6] 'With a more marked, openly erotic display of the heroine involving actual dance as opposed to romantic songs with sensual movement, a number of devices were deployed to essentially excuse or justify erotic display, and disavow the voyeuristic gaze' (Kasbekar 2003: 286–308). I would like to contend that creative pretexts such as masquerade/impersonations, meta-performances and fantasy sequences functioned as exonerating textual devices, definitively contributing to Madhuri's 'clean', innocent-yet-sensual image that has endured over time.

First, impersonation and masquerade were convenient and popular strategies deployed to justify overt representations of female sexuality, and the pleasures derived from beholding a masquerading star. When *Khalnayak* was released in August 1993, it was one of the biggest hits since *Sholay* (*Embers*, 1975), and instantly became controversial, triggering censor waves and moral panics over the 'bold' representation of female sexuality.[7] Much of the controversy revolved around the highly suggestive, *double entendre* song picturisation 'Choli ke Peeche Kya Hai', which was based on a bawdy Rajasthani folk song. The song featured Madhuri, as a feisty undercover sub-inspector named Ganga, masquerading as a dancer in an attempt to seduce the villain Ballu (Sanjay Dutt) in his den of thugs, and to deliver him to her lover, the righteous police officer, Ram (Jackie Shroff).

The erotic dance sequence, featuring close-ups of the heaving bosom, buttocks and thrusting pelvic gyrations of Madhuri, attired in the (in)famous cleavage-enhancing vibrant *choli* (blouse), pushed the boundaries in terms of its overt expression of female sexuality and lustful desire. Clare Wilkinson-Weber suggests that 'the masquerade is the very point at which her star persona asserts itself most vigorously … . Her costume is meticulously made and precisely fitted, so that she can do this to the best of her ability' (2014: 97). Through editing and suggestive cinematography, Ballu and his men

Trademark seductive dance movements in the controversial 'Choli' song picturisation featured in *Khalnayak* (1993)

are positioned as voyeurs within the diegetic space, passively viewing an erotic dance spectacle unfold before their lustful eyes, replicating the voyeuristic spectatorial 'male gaze' of theatrical audiences. As Jyotika Virdi reminds us, 'the song and dance sequences stand in for sex scenes. The focus is particularly on the heroine, the fetishized female sexualized through close attention to her costumes, graceful body movements, and carefully angled shots that heighten scopic pleasure' (2003: 146).

Rosie Thomas notes how 'female sexuality as cipher of purity was up for grabs as Madhuri Dixit flaunted her torso in a defiant provocation of the restrictive codes around male and female sexuality' (Thomas 2014: 286). 'Choli ke Peechey's' circulation independent of the film combined with Madhuri Dixit's star persona enable us to read the song as an articulation of female desire by a knowing female subject, thereby generating a space for women's sexual agency' (Mehta 2011: 184).

Music and cassette technology played instrumental roles in the success (and controversial nature) of the film and song. The lyrics of 'Choli ke Peeche', apparently offending the sensitivity of 'decent' middle-class audiences, were perceived as 'obscene' and 'vulgar' by some sections of society, and the song was banned on Doordarshan and All India Radio, its notoriety ensuring that the song became the number one hit of the year (ibid.), and filling the coffers of its music distributor, Tips Industries. In keeping with the general practice of deploying music to publicise the film, Tips first released the song as part of the film's audio cassette, in advance, when the film was in production; then it was televised as a music video, created from publicity clips from the film, on cable and satellite television; and finally the public encountered this infamous song in the film itself in theatrical halls (Mehta 2011: 196). Thus, the suggestive song could be heard blaring from radios and cassette players, causing panic and fear in some quarters that it would lead to 'eve-teasing' (euphemism for sexual harassment), moral degradation, and an irreparable erosion of Indian values and culture.

However, when Madhuri first heard the song, she did not think of it as obscene or vulgar nor did she 'think of the lyrics so literally. The beat was good and the tune catchy' and it didn't 'disturb' her. She recalls, 'People came down very heavily on that song. It was uncalled for. For this particular song we needed naughty, not vulgar gestures' (Kalarikal 1996: 54). When asked if she thought the sequence was obscene, she felt that the song picturisation, 'a difficult dance to do', was 'naughty but not vulgar in any way'. She mentioned the song's folksy Rajasthani origin as one typically sung at functions and weddings; the importance of the context of the scene referring to her character as 'in the garb of a prostitute'; and the intentions of the director and choreographer which, according to her, were decidedly not vulgar (Pradhan 1993: 12).

Thomas observes that, 'with the song and ... plot device of the undercover cop, the Ganga character pushed the split persona of the Hindi film heroine further than almost any film before;' the tough-cop persona reminiscent of 1980s avenging woman roles while the sexy Ganga avatar engendered the persona of the provocative heroine; and asserts, 'from this point on, distinctions between heroine and vamp began to crumble as item numbers became de rigueur for the female stars' (ibid.: 287). Virdi concurs, pointing out that

> in the 1980s the sexualized Hindi film heroine was no longer punished as was the phallic vamp for satisfying specular desires. Female stars' feigned lack of awareness of their bodies gave way to consciously teasing the limits of, and the pleasure in, "showing". (2003: 174)

The heroine lost many inhibitions during the decade. Ranjani Mazumdar, citing Dixit's provocative dance numbers in *Tezaab* and *Khalnayak*, noted

> the earlier binary oppositions, so dear to the nationalist imaginary, had ceased to hold. The heroine now occupied the space of the vamp through a process marked by a public display of desire and an entirely new discourse of sexuality that threatened the old boundaries. (2007: 90)

The pretext of impersonation proffered the masquerading star licence to be overtly sexual without tainting her 'good girl' reputation. According to Sohini Ghosh, 'by allowing female protagonists to masquerade as someone else song sequences often become spaces of resistance' (2000: 167). Therefore, understandably 'feminist scholars have used masquerade as a critical-theoretical concept to discuss the performative aspects of gender, in particular femininity …' (Srinivas 2009: 180).[8] Liberating and conveniently permissive in disguise, Madhuri as Ganga puts on a bold act for a greater cause – to uphold the law. Moreover, the common device of the masquerade, often adopted in melodrama (the default super genre of popular Indian cinema), affords the spectators considerable pleasure when they recognise 'a star in the disguise of the character' (ibid.).

There is a hierarchy of knowledge as the spectator is 'made aware of the legitimate reasons for the pretense' and knows that when the act ends, 'moral equilibrium will be restored' (Mehta 2011: 163). In fact, Madhuri 'liked the film's plot because the girl's character was interesting. She takes a stand. She is determined to help her fiancé and at the same time stick to her values' (Kalarikal 1996: 54). Therefore, she is 'in reality' a 'good woman', who, out of a sense of duty to her fiancé, stages an erotic dance act. As Monika Mehta suggests, 'Our privileged knowledge about Ganga's ruse and the extradiegetic knowledge that Dixit is a virtuous daughter generate a moral cocoon' (ibid.: 164).

Second, meta-performance was another popular strategy in exonerating the transgressive actions and behaviour of female characters whereby the actress/star was cast in the role of a professional or amateur performer, actor, singer, or dancer/courtesan.[9] The unwilling professional stage performer, she could be the victim of circumstances, subjected to parental coercion to dance in public, or forced into the occupation in order to survive. Due to the social stigma attached to women dancing for money in public, there had to be a strong justification for her choice of occupation. In the specific case study of Madhuri, 'duty and duress help to explain away the display of the heroine's dancing body, and a significant amount of narrative time is invested in establishing that the character played by Dixit is to be considered a good girl' who would normally never dance (provocatively or otherwise) on stage (Iyer 2015: 142). Madhuri as Mohini in *Tezaab* is forced to perform publicly for a paying audience by her avaricious father while she longs to give it all up for love and marriage. *Saajan* (in which Madhuri gets second billing before Salman Khan in the opening credits) is another example of meta-performance – Madhuri as Pooja (meaning 'worship' in Hindi) is an amateur stage performer first introduced via a musical segment as she plays the piano in front of a diegetic audience, a trademark introduction to the actress through her favourite star vehicle of the song and dance/music segment.

Produced by Gulshan Kumar and Super Cassettes Industries Ltd, the underrated *Sangeet* (*Music*, 1992) failed at the box office, although it was a favourite film of Madhuri's (Kalarikal 1996: 56). Another example of the meta-performance device, the star is cast in a double role as an elderly woman Nirmala who gives up dancing, and as a younger, blind danseuse Sangeeta who is oblivious to the skimpy clothes she wears when she dances on stage – an ironic self-reflexive commentary on Madhuri's own racy on-screen outfits. A poor, helpless, seemingly orphaned girl, Sangeeta performs bawdy dances for crowds of lascivious men because she is a victim of circumstances but the narrative goes to great lengths to establish that she actually desires to learn *accha nachh* (good dance).

Lajja is yet another example of meta-performance – Madhuri's character is the spirited thespian, Janki, who enacts the roles of Madhubala's Anarkali in the classic 1960 film song 'Pyar Kiya to Darna Kya' ('I Have Loved, So What Is There to Fear?') from *Mughal-e-Azam* (Emperor of the Mughals); and of the goddess Sita. *Devdas* is an exemplary instance of meta-performance, the role of Chandramukhi, a lovelorn courtesan, an ideal vehicle to showcase Madhuri as a dancing star. Receiving second billing ahead of Aishwarya Rai (as Paro), it is a significant departure from her customary roles. In her younger days Madhuri would have been cast as Paro but was now making way for the next female superstar-in-waiting – passing the baton to the next generation. The reigning queen of the 1990s, Madhuri's iconic superstar status in 2002 allowed her the freedom to be an overt embodiment of seduction and desire. There was no longer any need for pretexts and exonerating narrative devices to justify the expression of female sexuality, and no longer were the representation or expression of intimate emotions relegated to dream and fantasy spaces. Cameo roles also afforded her another opportunity to showcase her talent as a dancing star - as she does in *Bade Miyan, Chote Miyan* (*Elder Brother, Younger Brother*, 1998), co-starring with Amitabh Bachchan and Govinda, which generated much press attention for the two then fading superstars; or as an erotic fantasy (in *Dharavi*) without any undue concern about offending anyone or tainting reputations.

Another common exonerating textual device is the dream/ fantasy sequence, a veritable cliché in commercial Hindi cinema, wherein Madhuri is represented as 'the perfect vehicle for 1980s and 1990s male fantasy' (Bamzai 2008: 17) – the Indian male's wet dream. For instance, the highly erotic 'Dhak Dhak' (heartbeat) song picturisation in *Beta* is unambiguously framed as the sexual fantasy of the hero, suggesting that it did 'not "really" happen, meaning there is no conflict with the heroine's purity' (Morcom 2011: 169). In the controversial documentary, *Father, Son and Holy War* (1994), its critically acclaimed director Anand Patwardhan refers to the 'Dhak Dhak' song as 'epitomising male fantasy'. The sequence begins after the hero, Raja (Anil Kapoor) stares longingly at a photograph of Saraswati (Madhuri) and once over, Raja awakens in a haystack. Furthermore, the dialogue explicitly refers to it as a *sapna*/dream. Therefore, this Madhuri trademark dream sequence, which earned her the moniker 'Dhak Dhak Girl', unequivocally suggests, through formal elements, that it is the male protagonist's lust that generates this fantasy of her dancing in a brazen manner, thereby justifying and excusing any obscenity or vulgarity on her part.

Seductive body movements, heavy breathing, thrusting thighs and buttocks, and heaving breasts, captured in 'dirty' close-ups, by the

The iconic 'Dhak-Dhak' (Heartbeat) song picturisation from *Beta* (1992)

cinematographer Baba Azmi characterised the 'dance vocabulary' of this memorably erotic routine, one that decidedly blurred the boundaries between heroine and vamp. As Morcom points out,

> in most film songs (barring perhaps devotional ones), the use of costumes, camera work (revealing or magnifying angles and close ups), movement/ dance, and expression ... emphasize[d] a sensuous/erotic view of the heroine ... not found in the main part of the narrative.[10] (Morcom 2011: 168)

Despite its notoriety, Madhuri, however, 'didn't find anything vulgar about *Dhak, dhak*', although she says she 'did get a lot of flak for it. But it's a dance that men and women enjoyed in a big way .... In *Dhak, dhak* things like the orange lighting effect gave it a totally different impact' (Pradhan 1993: 12). She reveals that the song picturisation was shot after the film got a release date in one night and without any rehearsals.

> Baba Azmi [the cinematographer] had got so charged, he screamed at us, "... Chalo ek ganda sa close up dete hain" (come on, let me give a dirty close up), she recollects, "but I don't think there was anything dirty in that song picturisation." According to her, "it wasn't vulgar at all," asserting that she had "full faith in Sarojji" [Khan]. (Kalarikal 1996: 54)

For Gahlot, 'Madhuri's facial expressions in "Dhak Dhak" were very provocative – they were total Saroj Khan' (personal communication, June 2013).

Bappi Lahiri's disco-influenced hit-song sequence 'Tamma Tamma' was another instance of a dream sequence, from a precursor text to *Khalnayak* entitled *Thanedaar*, starring Sanjay Dutt as the villain Brijesh aka Birju (an intertextual reference to the iconic role played by Dutt's superstar father in *Mother India*) and Madhuri as his girlfriend, Chanda (*moon*). Her *Dharavi* (a 1992 off-beat art film by Sudhir Mishra) dream appearances in a seductive red sari are exemplary – dominating space on the film's official poster and on DVD covers. She inhabits a dream-like, surreal, fantastic space as a taxi driver's (Om Puri) fantasy, affording him immense relief and welcome distraction from a grim life in the eponymous slums of Bombay (Mumbai). As the taxi driver, Raj Karan's fantasy, Madhuri appears thrice in the same alluring red sari, twirling

Madhuri's guest appearance as a male fantasy featured on *Dharavi*'s (1992) official wall poster

and smiling, lying on a bed of yellow flowers, and sitting atop a taxi. The film opens with a fictitious Madhuri–Anil Kapoor movie 'Shahar Ka Shahenshah' screened in a tent in the slum named Dharavi. On her first appearance, cheered by loud whistling and cat-calling diegetic spectators, she quite literally sets the screen ablaze as an outbreak of fire causes mayhem among the slum dwellers. She appears again, this time on a communal television screen, in the famous dream sequence from *Dil*, starring opposite a newcomer named Aamir Khan.

Fashioning a star: Costume, fashion, style

Madhuri's costuming in song picturisations played a seminal role in the construction of her stardom. She wore audacious costumes that could transfigure a skinny girl into a voluptuous woman. Much as with the 1920s superstar Sulochana, Madhuri's films 'tended to project an overall atmosphere of glamour and an aura of the fashionable' while her 'on-screen fashion styles were widely emulated by middle-class women' (Bhaumik 2005: 92). *Screen* described Madhuri as 'the actress with an amazing malleability to fit into any costume and any role with consummate ease, the girl who manages to look different each time' (1990: 26). For Rachel Dwyer, she was one of several stars who was always a top trendsetter (2000: 188).

The tight-fitting, skimpy pink outfit worn in 'Ek Do Teen' in *Tezaab*; the 'Dhak Dhak' orange sari in *Beta*; the embroidered *ghagara choli* (skirt blouse) in *Khalnayak*, which triggered a wave of censorship; the iconic purple satin sari heavily embellished with crystals, matched with a backless blouse in *HAHK*, cheap imitations of which could be found in shopping centres and bazaars of urban India, sparking off a fashion craze; and the Manish Malhotra-designed chiffon saris from Yash Chopra's *DTPH* – each of these iconic costumes engendered powerfully affective recall values, leaving an indelible visual impact. Indeed, Madhuri's costumes, especially those worn in song and dance segments, were intrinsic to her stardom.

One of Bollywood's most iconic costumes, that inspired a fashion trend, was the shimmering purple sari, with heavy embroidery in *HAHK*, and the heavy *kundan* jewellery worn by Madhuri Dixit became so popular that every second Indian wedding saw the look replicated. Indeed, imitation is the best form of flattery and fan homage to a star. As Dwyer notes, indicative of the huge influence of *filmi* fashion on Indian society, 'this dress became one of the most copied items from the films … with girls asking their tailors to make them this outfit for family functions' (2000: 188). The look fuelled many enterprises, among them Barbie dolls in a similar purple sari flooded the market. The film also started the trend of backless *cholis*, making their creator Anna Singh the most celebrated designer of the decade. This look inspired many film-makers and was copied decades later in such films as the romantic comedy *Shirin Farhad Ki Toh Nikal Padi* (*Shirin and Farhad Made It*, 2012) (Nivas 2012). Wilkinson-Weber notes,

> all the examples of copied costumes are described as garments worn by the actor, not by the character. Rarely, if ever, does one hear of someone copying 'Nisha's' outfits from *Hum Aapke Hain Koun …!*, which would imply that emulation is focused on re-creating, via dress, a semblance of the character. Instead, the talk is of 'Madhuri's sari' or 'Madhuri's *lehenga*.' That a garment can be, at the same time, joined to a celebrity body and separable from it (to be worn by someone else) speaks to the ability of the audience to engage in the film's imaginary elements while recognizing that these elements derive from a material, physical reality that can be appropriated. (2014: 163)

Significantly, both official *HAHK* posters, in English and Hindi, feature Madhuri wearing the iconic purple satin sari and backless 'choli', the costuming becoming an easy identifier and promotional tool for the film.

Madhuri's *HAHK* (1994) iconic purple sari featured on Hindi and English-language official wall posters

As an image and memory, the costumes in which Madhuri danced hold a special significance, and a unique visual recall for generations of cinemagoers. Her dance and the costume in which she dances are inextricably linked in the memories of Indian audiences.

This is evident from recalling her most iconic costumes – the famous little pink outfit in *Tezaab*'s 'Ek Do Teen,' the seductive orange, sarong-style sari in 'Dhak Dhak' from *Beta*; the scandalous *ghagra choli* in *Khalnayak*; the aforementioned *HAHK* purple sari, and green *lengha choli*; the *DTPH* chiffon saris and *salwar kameezes*, designed by Manish Malhotra; and more recently, the 'Ghaghara' from the eponymous item number in *Yeh Jawaanai Hai Deewani* (*This Youthfulness Is Crazy*, 2013). Moreover, stars like Madhuri were

> more likely to drive fashion trends via a degree of play with the silhouette, fabric, and decorative features of saris, *salwar kameezes, ghagaras*, and the like than they were through wearing striking, but for most Indian women unwearable, Western styles. (Wilkinson-Weber 2014: 115)

These resplendent, ethnic Indian costumes, accentuating Madhuri's image of the quintessential traditional Indian woman, complemented her rounder, fuller physiognomy, and created a glamorous vision of grace, beauty, and poise. Rarely remembered in Western dress, she was perceived as the epitome of Indian femininity and elegance for her sartorial choices, especially one in particular – the ethnic chic, sexed up, village-belle costume that evolved into her trademark outfit (Dwyer 2000: 185). Additionally, her characters typically wore accessories, such as heavy silver folksy jewellery, namely, bangles, necklaces, anklets, nose-rings, 'tiklis' (worn along the middle parting of the head); regionally specific 'bindis' (decorative dots on foreheads), Madhuri's being famed for her half-moon 'bindis' typical of Maharashtrians; and the traditional hairstyle of wholesome heroines – long flowing hair imbued with erotic connotations.

> Dressing in liberating, permissive, and incongruous outfits meant that disguising the star in a costume [had] the paradoxical effect of reinforcing the star's allure. The return to more appropriate dress and the reinforcement of the message that disguise is mere appearance, not the outward form of moral sensibilities, tend to authenticate the validity of the star (Wilkinson-Weber 2014: 58)

In 'Choli ke Peeche, Kya Hai' Madhuri wore her trademark, sexed up village-belle *ghagra choli*, a disguise that, 'while never erasing the star, nevertheless demand[ed] that he or she assume an appearance and demeanor that [were] alien to his or her standard persona' (ibid.: 97). Although, as noted by Dwyer, her head was initially covered, 'the camera's close-ups on her heaving breasts and her naked back dispelled any suggestion of modesty,' in contrast to her 'real' character who wore staid 'khaki' police uniforms (2000: 185).

The heroine typically underwent numerous costume changes, the bigger the star the more changes, thus showcasing the star's 'adaptability' in looking good in a range of fashion styles, and 'her ability to don or remove clothes as masquerade' (Dwyer 2000: 186). Downright bizarre, impractical costumes in garish colours could be justified by the surreal and illogical nature of fantasies, the only directive being that fashion and hairstyles should be memorable to audiences. One outstanding example of outlandish costumes in fantasy/dream sequences, not meant for everyday wear, is Madhuri's (Madhu) costuming in the fantasy dance sequence that is prominently featured on the poster of *Dil*. The attires were described by Virdi as 'dressed in spectacular western fairy-tale-style prince and princess outfits: Madhu in flowing blue robes and glistening diamonds …' (2003: 88). Her flamboyant, piled up headgear is typical of a kind of 'freewheeling bricolage … emblematic of certain trends in 1980s costume that can be identified in other parts of the world' (Wilkinson-Weber

Flamboyant costuming in the dream sequence from *Dil* (1990)

2014: 111). Furthermore, it is a good example of *filmi* costuming, in other words, a dress that is 'flashy, excessive, or revealing, and frequently all three' (ibid.: 4); song and dance sequences being particularly 'wide open for bold fashion statements, since forays into imaginative worlds are fodder for costume spectacles that owe far less to realism than do a film's other scenes' (ibid.: 101).

Historically, costuming has been a marker of character and class, and is often a yardstick used to distinguish the heroine from the vamp in popular Hindi cinema. As Madhuri's defence of her character's miniskirts in *Raja* reveals, 'the clothes set the tone for the character. The girl in *Raja* was very bold, almost brazen. She was outspoken and brash. So she would naturally be wearing a mini', apart from asserting that it was a true reflection of reality (Garimella 1995: 26). 'In DTPH, in which she plays Pooja, a dreamy amateur dancer who lives for love, she had a complete makeover, upgraded from middle-class to posh' (Bamzai 2008: 23–4). According to Dwyer, each of Madhuri's costumes designed by Manish Malhotra cost Rs. 25,000 and she had fifty costume changes. It was 'one of the most striking uses of the salwar-khamees … where they were worn by the "traditional" heroine' in contrast to the other sportswear-clad heroine. Pooja wore Western clothes on holiday, when she slept, and while performing on stage. 'The outfits have much transparent material, are cleavage-revealing and the scarf is used more for pictures of billowing material than for modesty' (2000: 185). According to its director, Yash Chopra,

> The only problem was to create a new look for Madhuri. Since she has done nearly 100 films, she has gone through every kind of look conceivable. We arrived at a subtle Indian look for her which I think presents her in a new light ('Best Film – Yash Chopra: DTPH' 1998: 58)

Even her costuming was mentioned in film reviews of DTPH: 'The intangible lightness of touch wraps you in a silky embrace like one of Madhuri's pastel chiffon *odhnis* (scarves) fluttering like a visual leitmotif in the film [...]' (Rao 1997: 10).

I have argued in this chapter that useful creative textual devices such as the masquerade/impersonation, meta-performance and fantasy sequence, reinforced by a 'wholesome' off-screen persona, assisted Madhuri in consistently maintaining a 'clean', unsullied, innocent-yet-sensual image, sheltering her from any charges of obscenity or vulgarity while introducing an unprecedented level of sensuality to popular Hindi film dance.

4 FROM STAR TO CELEBRITY

Millennial Bollywood: New industrial contexts, markets and media

This chapter examines the millennial reinvention of the Madhuri text as she transitioned from a film star to a transmedia celebrity, wherein dance remained a salient leitmotif. Her new media avatars emerged as she negotiated the challenges of a constantly evolving media terrain vastly different from the one she had been familiar with during her reign as the queen of commercial Hindi cinema. This period was marked by the seismic and radical reorganisation, restructuring and corporatisation of the Bombay film industry as it transformed from a regionally defined film entity into a global media industry as a corollary of 1990s neo-liberal economic policies of the Indian state; the convenient co-option of South Asian diasporas within 'the global Indian family' (Punathambekar 2013: 29) by the state, materially, financially, and imaginatively; and the government's long-awaited conferral of 'industry' status to Bollywood in 1998. The conjunction of these factors engendered the uneven, complex, and problematic emergence of a behemoth known (often pejoratively) as 'Bollywood', an artistic, stylistic, and industrial formation distinct from popular Hindi cinema, its antecedent.

The film industry in its bid to emerge as a global player distanced itself from dubious, unregulated financial investors by seemingly adopting more transparency in accountancy, opting for loans and investments from nationalised and multinational banks, and by generally cleaning up its act in order to attract international funding, tie-ups, and co-productions. A narrative of convergence of film, television, and new media has characterised the remarkable augmentation of India's mediascape, with the insertion of corporate fund managers and investors, MBA-flaunting marketing and advertising executives, and enterprising and opportunistic diasporic internet entrepreneurs leading to newly emergent and available transnational flows and transmedia circuits of capital, labour, and distribution and exhibition platforms (Punathambekar 2013).

India's digital revolution has dramatically transformed the media and communications, and entertainment sectors. It is one of the fastest-expanding and largest markets for smartphones and tablets in the world, due to the growth of its aspirational and acquisitive middle-class population. Cellular network companies such as Reliance Industries Ltd and Bharti Airtel (the leading Indian mobile network operator) now offer high-speed, affordable, and reliable 4G broadband services to urban households. The major driver propelling the expansion of internet usage among the young generation is online entertainment including gaming, music, and cinema. As broadband and cellular data connectivity spreads and improves, streaming and downloading film content and television shows are becoming increasingly viable options. The impact of digitisation on the Bombay film industry, and its deeply entrenched and influential star system, has been profound.

The overall work environment, ethic, and practices of the Bombay film industry have changed over the past decade. The corporates have introduced a professional sensibility and structure, and a sense of discipline and preparedness in terms of the availability of a script, adhering to a production schedule, and cutting cost. Films are completed in a shorter period of time and nearly every aspect of filming is planned ahead of time, from costumes to hairstyles.

Previously, it was more ad hoc and spontaneous in terms of shooting, scripting, and production schedules and could take years to complete projects, with some even abandoned midway for lack of funds. Technically, digital cameras and state-of-the-art equipment are now available; foreign crews often collaborate on special effects, and action and stunt choreography; and the budgets have escalated. The working conditions are more conducive for actors and, according to Madhuri, 'it's a different generation of actors and actresses; they are much more ambitious, they are go-getters and that's good' (Kulkarni 2008: 84).

From film star to transmedia celebrity

Although many stars are popular for only a limited time, being vulnerable to the notoriously fickle tastes and fashion of their audiences and fans, in certain instances as with Madhuri, 'stars seem to transcend historical fashions, enjoying continuing popularity over different periods of time [although] the image of a star is nevertheless still historically transformed' (McDonald 2000: 8). The Madhuri Dixit of the 1990s is not the same as the Madhuri of the post-2000 era as her star text transforms over time, and is thus examined within a set of changing cultural and historical contexts and circumstances.

Celebrity culture in India

Madhuri, her husband and her corporate team have expended considerable effort to devise strategies for adapting and tailoring her brand to exploit the new culture of celebrity. 'Stardom is only a particular form of celebrity' (Prasad 2014: 19), arguably the most exclusive, rare breed whose work in films has elevated them to celebrity status can be called 'stars', occupying the top position in the hierarchy of celebrities. As Madhava Prasad notes, 'Broadly, film actors seem to qualify for the title of star, whereas celebrity seems to be a phenomenon arising in the context of the mass media, especially television' (ibid.). The exponential rise in the numbers of celebrities since the mid-1990s is a corollary of India's embrace of a capitalist economy after decades of socialism and a mixed economy. Before economic liberalisation, paving the way for the entry of a plethora of private cable/satellite television channels, the conditions did not exist for the full exploitation and commercialisation of star value for marketing purposes. No one underestimates the income-generating, fundraising power and clout of celebrities, functioning as marketing tools for media entrepreneurs, film producers, marketers, and television programmers who seek celebrity involvement in projects in order to attract and build audiences and investment, and to endorse and advertise products (Turner 2007: 193). As Graham Turner notes, 'Celebrity also makes money for the individual concerned ... in two ways. While they are cultural workers and are paid for their labour, celebrities are also "property" (Dyer 1986: 5) ... they are a financial asset to those who stand to gain from their commercialisation ...' (2007: 193).

Observing 'the meek surrender of the Bombay film industry's star assets to the television and advertising industries in the space of just over a decade', Prasad asserts that, 'Bollywood' has turned itself into

> an appendage of the consumer goods industry via advertising ... the mainstream commercial film industry ... is getting absorbed into the larger cultural economy of consumer goods advertising and related areas. Advertising in India, backed by the steady inflow of global capital, has the sort of economic muscle that the film industry could never dream of. It is only by making peace with it that the latter has any prospects of increasing its own money power. (2014: 22–3)

In short, 'Bollywood stars, given the opportunity, have voluntarily relinquished the exclusivity of film stardom and embraced the benefits of a more widely investible celebrity', imitating 'the domination of all-purpose celebrity over stardom as aesthetic specialisation' prevalent in East Asian countries such as South Korea (ibid.: 23). Similar to the situation in the United States, millennial India has a plethora of A-list and B-list celebrities from the world of cinema, television, fashion, sports (especially cricket, which has historically dominated Indian sports even before liberalisation), politics, literature, and business. Furthermore, in this celebrity-obsessed culture where fame is transient, there is a constant search for the next big star in the entertainment industries through televised talent and game shows, contests, reality television shows, and beauty pageants. Some celebrities who find lasting fame (such as A-list Bollywood stars and top cricketers) become 'brand names as well as cultural icons or identities … and they represent the achievement of individualism – the triumph of the human and the familiar – as well as its commodification and commercialisation' (Turner, Bonner and Marshall cited in Redmond and Holmes 2007: 190).

Madhuri's brand name continues to be associated with dance in all its diverse forms and exhibition platforms as her recent films, television appearances, and her virtual avatars demonstrate. Iyer astutely points out that 'her continued fame as a dancer-actress opens up and challenges conventional trajectories of female stars' careers in Hindi cinema'. Her so-called 'comeback' film *Aaja Nachle*, about a non-resident Indian dancer returning to India to save a theatre in her village, was 'clearly designed as a vehicle for her dancing talents in that it has extratextual resonances with Dixit's life and comes across as a paean to her and to popular Hindi film dance' (Iyer 2015: 151). Although it flopped, Madhuri, the only star in the film, selected it because its concept had touched a nerve. She said she loved the fact that the film was about a woman 'who leaves her country and goes somewhere else, makes a life for herself … then finds out that whatever she was passionate about is crumbling and she has to come back, and she has to fight for that culture' (Sen 2014). For the first time, Madhuri

> not only performs but also creates; she has moved from being the disciple to becoming the guru and teacher … in keeping with her … being celebrated on TV shows and in award ceremonies as the leading exponent of popular Hindi film dance. (Iyer 2015: 153)

This was also a rare mature role appropriate for Madhuri's age, it being a challenge finding substantial roles for older female stars in the Hindi film industry due to deep-seated bias for young heroines in their early 20s, cast for their physicality rather than talent, thus pandering to Bollywood's predilection for objectifying women.

Ageing celebrity discourse

The 'ageing female star' in Bollywood faces particular challenges owing to double standards for male and female stars. While male actors enjoy longevity and clout – the three Khans, Aamir, Shah Rukh and Salman have been at the top for twenty years and 'continue to demand serious paychecks and progressively younger heroines' (Chopra 2011b), actresses have much shorter career spans, especially after they turn thirty or marry. The travails of the ageing female Bollywood star exceed their American counterparts. Although there is gender bias and ageism in Hollywood, Bollywood is yet to produce the equivalent of Meryl Streep, Helen Mirren, Judi Dench, Jane Fonda, and Sally Field. Shabana Azmi comes closest to representing an established older female actor, continuing to act despite her age, in roles as varied as that of a witch, don, affectionate mother, and manipulative politician. However, as an art-house actress and not a mainstream Bollywood star, Azmi does not have the commercial cachet required to make producers and film-makers change the way they write roles, or the rules of the game.

In fact as early as 1998, when Madhuri had just reached her thirties, *Movie* magazine printed scathing ageist remarks on how it is 'an inevitable, irrevocable law of the youth-worshipping industry that after a heroine hovers around 30, she hits the skids. Moreover, the plumper Madhuri grew, the slimmer her dances got …' (Kothari 1998: 18). It reported someone from the industry cynically remarking, 'you can't override the age factor. There's little interest value in seeing Madhuri do typical heroine roles which she's already done so many of, so filmmakers seek novelty in other younger heroines …' (ibid.). As Madhuri's dance mentor, Saroj Khan notes, 'Bollywood is a tough place, tougher for actresses and toughest for married actresses who want to make a comeback.' This is not the sort of industry benevolent enough to allow 'a returning diva her old place at the top' (Srivastava 2013).

Considerable pressure on female stars to look perennially youthful forces many to resort to cosmetic surgery, Botox, dermal fillers, rhinoplasty surgery, and other procedures. Madhuri in interviews has said that she is not against plastic surgery, referring to it as a 'boon' to many in both Hollywood and Bollywood. Her cosmetic surgery is evident, and a cursory internet search reveals that it is a subject of considerable gossip and media speculation. Eyebags, sagging skin, and wrinkles have given way to a tight jawline, angular nose, and lifted eyes through popular procedures such as a facelift and cheek refinement, nose job, and lip augmentation, and the use of Botox to make her appear wrinkle-free. In September 2016, it was widely reported in the media that Madhuri had been hospitalised in the US for a shoulder injury, a sure sign of an ageing body under stress, and the wear and tear of labour precipitating the inevitable breakdown of the dancing body. Although this might have been expected as Madhuri had just entered her fifties, it was still surprising since it revealed an uncharacteristic chink in the armour of someone known for her age-defying fitness, excellent physique, and healthy lifestyle.

As an ageing celebrity whose stardom is no longer primarily dependent on cinema, there is added pressure to maintain a high profile and 'visibility'. So great is the value of visibility that the manufacturing and marketing of celebrities now reach into business, sports, entertainment, religion, the arts, politics, academics, medicine, and law.

> Visibility is what every aspiring actor wants and every unknown professional seeks. This is the new world of industrialized celebrity … in which individuals … can be elevated to a level of visibility unimaginable at any other time – and be compensated with imaginable rewards. (Reiner, Kotler and Stoller cited in Redmond and Holmes 2007: 5)

Indeed, no publicity is bad publicity any more in this era of 24/7 news media coverage and the ubiquity of social media as celebrities compete for constant media attention, often planting false stories, rumours, and 'scandals' to ensure maximum exposure. '"The value of visibility" has become a commodity in *its own right*, quite independent from "accomplishment, sacrifice, heroics"' (ibid.).

Reality television dance celebrity

'Television is the medium that imposes on all stars, from any realm of achievement, the common measure of commercial exploitability. In submitting to this common measure, stars agree to become celebrities' (Prasad 2014: 24). Complex and multifaceted industries are responsible for the production and circulation of celebrity that have increased exponentially in the last few decades in India (ibid.: 189). The Indian film stars' net worth and value gain significantly by their television and advertisement exploits. Reality television is one of the entertainment industries contributing to Madhuri's millennial reinvention. No longer just a film star, she has developed an expansive brand by taking advantage of the popularity of the reality-television genre (*Big Boss* (2006–), *Kaun Banega Crorepati* (*Who Wants to Be a Millionaire*, 2000–14), *Indian Idol* (2004–), *India's Got Talent* (2009–) to name a few), imported formats appropriated and adapted for Indian audiences. Thus, in Madhuri's case, 'a certain stage is reached in the career of a star image, after which films become mere appearances, manifestations, comparable to royalty's appearing before the public from the palace balcony' (ibid.: 26).

On 12 December 2010, when she appeared as a judge and dance guru on the dance reality show *Jhalak Dikhhla Jaa 4*, India's version of BBC's *Strictly Come Dancing*, aired on the privately owned channel Sony Entertainment Television, she made her formal transition from star to celebrity by entering the increasingly lucrative and popular world of Indian reality television. The media announced that 'Bollywood's favourite dancing queen is back. Madhuri Dixit is judging the dance reality show "Jhalak Dikhhla Jaa 4" along with item girl Malaika Arora Khan and choreographer Remo D'Souza.' The show was built around her celebrity status, evoking nostalgia for her past career. From the channel's publicity material and in the twenty-four episodes of the fourth season, it was evident that the spotlight was firmly on Madhuri. Episodes reprised her characters (such as *Tezaab*'s Mohini), legendary 1990s dance performances were restaged, and her chemistry with her former male co-stars Anil Kapoor and Shah Rukh Khan was reenacted. Her husband made an appearance, proposing to her again on national television during *Jhalak Dikhhla Jaa 6*, bolstering 'the good wife, loving mother' image that traditional Indian audiences would approve of and identify with, while demonstrating her husband's support for her late career, and that they were a loving couple in a strong marriage (thus dispelling rumours of a divorce).

In 2012 and 2013, Madhuri rejoined *Jhalak Dikhhla Jaa* 5 and *Jhalak Dikhhla Jaa 6* along with her co-judges Remo D'Souza, and Bollywood director-producer and talk-show host, Karan Johar, now telecast by the privately owned channel, Colors. Later on in 2014, the show was renewed for a seventh season, *Jhalak Dikhhla Jaa 7* and she returned to the judging panel for the fourth time with the same co-judges. Instead of heavy Indian clothes, during this season she wore a lot of Western apparel and experimented with new dance styles such as salsa, tango, and flamenco. According to her, she had turned to television because she loved dancing and it helped her connect with her fans, including those from a younger generation. She felt that 'the sky was the limit for actors' and believed they 'should be able to perform in any medium. With the Internet, the world has become a small place and there is so much to choose from. The audience learns so much from reality shows on TV' (Awaasthi 2014: 6). However, for various reasons speculated upon in the media, including declining popularity ratings, Madhuri decided against continuing for an eighth season, instead joining another reality show.

Jhalak Dikhhla Jaa was a shrewd strategic move in the reinvention of Madhuri's celebrity brand. The reality-television dance format provided an ideal self-reflexive platform to restage, revisit, and remind audiences of her 1990s superstardom while expanding her fan base among younger generations who were not born when she was at her peak. She was the 'star' attraction, the entire show revolving around her star persona as Bollywood's finest dancing diva and built on the recognition of her superstardom. Through nostalgia, memory, homages, and dance tributes by contestants and guests, her career milestones were a constant reference point. As Usha Iyer observes, every night 'with trademark moves – a coquettish raise of the eyebrow, a wanton toss of her head – or instructions to the show's participants on how to perfect that subtle swing of the hip', the prima donna of Hindi film dance 'activate[d] spectatorial memories of her dancing on television sets' (2015: 152). She revelled in paying tribute to her former self, her past career, and achievements – a grandiose exercise in self-congratulatory narcissism.

In 2016, she joined a new television dance reality show, *So You Think You Can Dance – Ab India Ki Baari (It's Now India's Turn)*,[1] as judge alongside choreographers Terence Lewis and Bosco Ceaser, telecast on ANDTV (&TV) India television channel. She found the format far more fascinating than that of *Jhalak* because it features ordinary people as opposed to stars. According to her, she 'felt good to be attached to this show and interact with the common man. They are passionate dancers who have made many sacrifices, didn't have family support but still didn't leave their passion for dance' (T2 Online April 2016). On 2 June 2018, Madhuri returned to television after a hiatus of two years as judge for a new reality show *Dance Deewane* (*Dance Madness*), broadcast on Colors (FirstPost, April 2018).

Dance with Madhuri (DWM) online: Use of internet and social media

Over the past few decades, digital and virtual media convergences, of the internet, the video-gaming industry, transnational cable channels, and the rapid growth and bi-directional media content outsourcing and visual effects companies have significantly transformed post-millennial Bombay film industry. There has been an exponential growth and penetration of satellite/cable and internet accessed by millennial Indians, largely urban, educated, aspirational youths, aware of global genres, and the latest media trends. Digital media has fundamentally transformed star and celebrity discourses in India. Online social media has reconfigured the visibility, accessibility, and interactivity of celebrities and fans. In the era of new media and transmedia intersections with traditional media, new kinds of fan interactivity and diffused star discourses have dramatically altered the construction of Bollywood stardom in the age of new media via Twitter, Facebook, Instagram, virtual chat rooms and message boards, fan websites and blogs, YouTube fan tributes, and official online star profiles as 'the Internet goes a long way towards continuing and further promoting the appeal of film stars' (McDonald 2000: 115).

As discussed in Chapter 2, 'television extended the presence of the film star system into the living room' (ibid.: 113), making Madhuri one of the first televisual stars of her generation. However, 'whilst television and print media continue to actively circulate the discourses of film stardom … the most rapid growth in the dissemination of those discourses has come with the widespread adoption of the Internet' (ibid.). The internet has 'expanded the existing discourses of stardom through decentring the production of star discourses', opening out to diverse sources the authorship of star discourses, and offering 'the opportunity for an interactive construction of star discourse that was not possible with previous channels of mass communication' (ibid.: 115).

In India 'by 2005–06, the Internet had certainly become a vital component of every film's career, with marketing executives and public relations agents ensuring that every film had a dedicated website and a tie-in with a dot.com company' (Punathambekar 2013: 114). Major studios 'explored various online marketing and distribution initiatives to reach overseas audiences', many sites exclusively targeting affluent Non-Resident Indian (NRI) diasporic communities. Rajat Barjatya, marketing manager at Rajshri Productions, declared that the web would be a 'multiplex with unlimited seats' (ibid.). Ananda Mitra refers to the virtual counterpart of Bollywood as 'Bollyweb', a global phenomenon transcending the territorial boundaries of the nation-state and its institutions, which is enormously popular with South Asian diasporas. He identifies five interlinked web-based resources via which Bollywood and its formidable star system assert a global virtual presence – institutional web pages, personal web pages, blogs, usenet groups, and chat rooms (2008: 269–76). Thus, the internet boom and the new/social media usage by Bollywood celebrities, and their fan bases, necessitate the radical reconfiguration of the discursive practices of stardom. Arguing that Bollyweb acts as a 'digital memory of Bollywood', Mitra mentions that a search for images of Madhuri Dixit ... yields 4,530 websites which in turn have multiple images of the actress. This is an alternative history that is being authored in the realm of the virtual, where the fans and the critics are creating a repertoire of texts, images, and sounds which could be preserved to create a networked digital history of Bollywood that would be much more textured than books and chronicles. (2008: 278)

Dancing fundamentally informs and underpins Madhuri's celebrity text. The Bollywood dancing diva is repackaged and branded for the consumption of a newer generation of audiences on convergent transmedia platforms as she extends her stardom into the boundless realms of the internet through the creation of RnM Moving Pictures Pvt. Ltd (http://www.rnmmovingpictures.com/) – a company founded by Madhuri and her husband, Dr Sriram Nene, that is the product of '30 years of hindi cinema experience and 30 years of technology and medical experience' (ibid.) Representing the efforts of its founders 'in producing world class media and content, it comprises of five verticals: Entertainment, Health, Lifestyle, Interactive and Gaming, all of which allow for synergy through innovation, interaction and content development' (ibid.). The company has created the significant digital products, MadhuriDixit-Nene.com website and the Madhuri Dixit apps across all iOS and Android devices as well as TopHealthGuru.Com, and DrNene.Com, to name a few.

Four products conceived exclusively to develop the Madhuri brand online are: MadhuriDixit-Nene.com, the official website for the star; Madz.Me, a portal for her newly launched clothing line for dancers and athletes; Bollyout, especially designed to create a 'cool combination of hit Bollywood signature steps with a caloric-determined fitness routine' that claims to 'ensure caloric burn, minimising the effort and maximising the fun quotient' (http://www.rnmmovingpictures.com/); and the pioneering online dance academy, 'Dance with Madhuri' (dancewithmadhuri.com), that proclaims (quoting Madhuri), 'Everyone has a spark inside them, our aim is to ignite it', and seeks to 'celebrate happiness, confidence and health with dance'.

Her official website, http://madhuridixit-nene.com/, powered by RnM Moving Pictures, provides the latest news on her and covers six topics, 'films,' 'dance', 'art', 'music', 'fashion', and 'health and beauty', featuring familiar images from *Filmfare* and *Vogue* magazines, a 'connect' tab that allows fans to send her messages ('I owe a great deal to my fans and love them dearly. Share your thoughts with me', see: http://madhuridixit-nene.com//connect), and links to her Facebook and Twitter accounts. It 'was created with the intention of connecting with fans on a broader spectrum and an initiative to return the love and support received through the years'. Madhuri entered the fashion world with her Madz clothing line, that 'represents her style sense and her approach towards life at its best'. Inspired by her online dance academy, DWM sports apparel line 'is designed to keep dancers and athletes in mind. The DWM shirts are engineered to be great for dancing and workouts. The goal is to make you look good and feel good while dancing/working out.' Her intention was to create a (Anon 2015) 'pret line of clothing that epitomised [her] approach to life: outstanding quality, great values, and good for everyone (sic)'. Madhuri is an excellent example of a global star who 'insist[s] on the primacy of individualism, more specifically a vision of individualism and subjectivity intertwined with the implementation of modernity and capitalism' (Meeuf and Raphael 2013: 5).

The uniquely conceived web portal Dance with Madhuri (DWM) claims to be 'the world's first celebrity backed, online, gamified dance academy [that] creates a place where we are allowed to learn, stay fit, and unite with the world' (http://www.dancewithmadhuri.com/misc/#!/misc/footer/aboutDWM). It further declares,

> Madhuri Dixit wanted to teach the world to dance and synchronize everyone's step. DWM acts as a metaphor for life, bringing together people

from around the world via dance' her dream being 'to spread the joy of dance.' In her words, 'Dance has been my passion since the age of 3, and it just grows stronger with time. DWM is an expression of my gratitude to my ever-loving fans who have contributed to what I am today.' The dance portal allows the learner to dance as if no one is watching, anytime, anywhere and with anyone. (ibid.)

It is a unique way to 'extend her legacy and attempts to bring her passion for dance to the world'. Her publicists envision 'reaching out to the masses through our digital, on-ground assets'. The web content constitutes dance-training videos and interactive coaching tools for five different dance categories, namely, Bollywood, Indian Classical and Folk, Club, Latin and Ballroom, Street Dancing, and Contemporary Jazz, offered at two skill levels of beginner and advanced. Gurus include Pandit Birju Maharaj, Remo D'Souza, Terence Lewis, and the dancing diva herself. Aside from dance routines, there are fitness regimes that include Dancercise, Body Conditioning Workout, Core Strengthening, Stretching, Tabata, Yoga, Functional Training, and Pilates.

DWM enables interactive chats, and the innovative 'Book a Dance Trainer' feature helps participants hire a trainer if they want to organise group dances for special personal and professional occasions and events by personalising their experiences. Learners may register as an individual or as an institution. Learning to Dance with/like Madhuri is a business enterprise as free subscriptions allow the learner to merely enrol and track progress, and to access a worldwide dance community while premium subscriptions for one, six, and twelve months for \$5, \$30 and \$60 respectively, allow the user to access advanced training features. India's premium satellite service Tata Sky launched on 14 December 2015, an initiative named Dance Studio, powered by Dance with Madhuri – a platform, where Tata Sky subscribers can be taught to dance by their favourite masters in the comfort of their living room. Madhuri's rationale behind her online dance academy is to 'contribute to making people aware by educating them about classical dance which is slowly being lost'. She opines that even masters of *kathak*, Bharatnatyam, experts in classical dancing say people don't want to learn it because they all want to become dancers overnight, an impossible feat without the knowledge of classical dance. 'Once you know classical, you can master any kind of dancing in the world' (Sen 2014).

Instead of the ageing star growing old, fading away and becoming 'invisible', Madhuri has been tirelessly reinventing, innovating, and adapting her brand to meet the challenges of a new media terrain that is decidedly different from the first phase of her career. Her youthful PR publicity management team is responsible for her hypervisibility, and for facilitating her reinvention across a plethora of social media (Facebook, Twitter) and promotional platforms. She has adopted a corporatised professional environment and a modus operandi that is geared towards maximising promotion, marketing, and publicity. For a fundamental shift has taken place within this historically marginalised and neglected sector of a now-rapidly corporatising Bombay film industry. Since marketing had become 'the new mantra in Bollywood' (Punathambekar 2013: 79), there has been a fundamental reconceptualisation of 'authoring hype' (ibid.: 81) which is no longer the exclusive domain of the producer and director; instead there has been 'a push for [a] more professionalized mode of film marketing and … emphasis on market research' (ibid.: 91); 'the reevaluation of film marketing and promotions as a distinct zone of creative and business practice … that demanded specialized knowledge' (ibid.: 100). A 2011 *Times of India* report entitled 'The Publicity Game' notes the prevaricating manner in which stars use the media to their advantage, whether it is for promotion of a film or to quell rumours of an affair. 'They swing between privacy and publicity but on their own terms' (Sinha 2011: 1). According to film-maker Mahesh Bhatt, 'visibility translates to mindshare which in turn translates to money'. For Komal Nahta, 'stars say and do things for the moment, as it suits them. They shouldn't be taken seriously' (ibid.). However, it is serious business for the numerous television channels all vying with each other for high TRPs (Television Rating Points), which often only film stars can guarantee in a country obsessed with cinema and celebrity.

Her Facebook page, https://www.facebook.com/MadhuriDixitNene/, managed by Madhuri and Team M at RnM Moving Pictures ensures that she stays constantly visible, accessible, and relevant by 'looking at new cool ways to connect' with her fans, for 'unlike the institutional authorship of newspapers and television, the Internet provides the individual with an instrument for communicating to a potential mass of readers and viewers' (McDonald 2000: 114). Her profile image is a gif of her applying make-up to her face and then smiling at the camera/viewer. Her page had 20 million likes in 2015, supports links to Twitter, Madz shop, YouTube, livestream, and presents photos, videos, and live video chats with fans. The Facebook page engenders and exploits feelings of nostalgia for her and for a bygone era by regularly posting videos of iconic song and dance sequences, and memorable moments from her hit films (for instance, prompting recall of her character Nisha in *HAHK* through montages of movie stills). It rekindles memories of her 1990s stardom, which keeps her legacy alive and relevant in public memory. Her Facebook publicists, calling themselves Team M, post short videos of her wishing fans well on significant national and religious occasions such as Independence Day, Diwali, Eid, and Onam, dance excerpts from television shows, and modelling glamorous fashion styles. Her Twitter handle is @MadhuriDixit and she has 6.77 million followers, having joined in November 2010. When she lived in the US her fans were dependent solely on her Twitter feeds and updates to stay informed about her. She says that through her tweets she is 'constantly finding ways to connect with the world. Loving the Twitter Universe!' Predictably, there are numerous photographs of her husband and herself (and occasionally of her two sons, Raayan and Arin), her international and domestic travels and events she has attended that successfully keep her in the public eye.

A case study of fandom: April Vuncannon aka 'Mayuri'

DWM has created an online dance community and Madhuri's stardom has truly

> become a 'glue' that can connect individuals across time and space, create identities, and hold them together. Stars grant modern people a sense of self and a sense of (placeless) place ... stardom provides significant emotional connections for otherwise relatively disconnected individuals (Kathleen Newman cited in Meeuf and Raphael 2013: 5).

This is exemplified by the following case study of the fan activities of a University of North Carolina Wilmington (UNCW) student, April Vuncannon, from High Point, North Carolina (NC), whose first introduction to Madhuri was through my popular Hindi Cinema course in 2010, prior to which she had little knowledge of Hindi cinema, the star, or of India, and yet within three years she would meet Madhuri twice in India, present her with a 'star', learn and perform *kathak* in an amateur US-based dance group, and unofficially adopt the Indian name of Mayuri. According to Vuncannon, 'Madhuri has a gift of motivating people to get up and dance' (personal communication, 2 June 2014). She travelled to 'India four times to learn the classical Indian dance Kathak, which is near and dear to Madhuriji. This passion of mine, found through her movies, has and keeps on bringing health and happiness.' She says that she is not alone, 'having met several classmates who came to dance after watching Madhuriji perform in *Devdas* (2002)'. According to her, Madhuri's 'talent (dance and acting), versatility, respectability and her approachable elegance' are the reasons for her stardom.

Vuncannon's extensive and intense fandom, much of which is internet based, has constituted watching almost all of Madhuri's movies, and *Dedh Ishqiya* and *Gulaab Gang* in theatres. She has followed

UNCW alumna April 'Mayuri' Vuncannon, a Madhuri fan, buying posters at Chor Bazaar, Mumbai

Jhalak Dikhhla Jaa 7 and visited the online dance academy, Dance with Madhuri; purchased magazines featuring Madhuri on the cover; collected newspaper articles which she then turned into a scrapbook; and followed Twitter feeds religiously. Vuncannon taught herself two dances from videos online, and was in the process of learning a third one; created a blog ('virtual shrines of star adoration' (McDonald 2000: 114)) that chronicled the sightings of Madhuri paraphernalia, books, posters, or pictures while travelling in India; followed Madhuri's

Facebook page to keep up with her current projects and 'read her wise yet light thoughts of the day'; and met 'strangers' she knew only from the internet, fans, described by her as 'kind, loyal and inclusive', who would celebrate the star's birthday by cutting cake, taking photographs, and sharing stories (personal communication, 2 June 2014).

Describing meeting Madhuri for the first time in 2012 as 'magical,' after the charity event 'Emeralds for Elephants' press conference at Mumbai's famous Taj Hotel, Vuncannon recalls how Madhuri was utterly taken aback when she bent down to touch her feet in a traditional mark of respect. In celebration of Madhuri's forty-fifth birthday, about fifteen fans, including Vuncannon, under the leadership of top fan Nitesh and the fan group 'The Empress' dedicated a star to her, presenting her with a plaque (that Vuncannon had brought from the US) on the set of *Jhalak Dikhhla Jaa*. Weeks later, a picture of the fan group with their favourite star, and an article, were published in the state (Marathi) paper (ibid.).

Fan ephemera created by Vuncannon includes an edited birthday video in celebration of Madhuri's forty-fourth birthday, also featured in Vuncannon's final video-editing project at university, both available on her YouTube channel. She entered a dance competition to win the chance to dance with Madhuri at the 15th IIFA awards in Tampa in 2014, and restaged a *lavani* mix of Madhuri's performances on *Jhalak Dikhhla Jaa* in 2014 and choreographed her own dances to her songs 'Kay Sera Sera' and 'Rang Saari Gulaabi' (All the Colours Are Rosy) while dancing as part of an amateur Bollywood dance group in NC's Triangle area; and finally, one of the reasons she is known as Mayuri is because it sounds similar to Madhuri. Asked if her fandom has changed over the years, Vuncannon offers an insight into the dynamic and evolving nature of a (super-)fan:

Most definitely! In the beginning, I would devote all my energies to following her life. I was young (insecure, unsure and timid) and needed a lively role model. But now, I have faith in myself and am embracing my own life! I still check in occasionally and whenever I do, it's like hearing about a favorite familiar friend and I smile (ibid.).

Transmedia celebrity work

> Celebrities, such as Madhuri, are now rarely restricted to a single medium, and the commercial and cultural value of the modern star or celebrity is seen to be predicated on their inter - and cross textual appeal … fuelling a debate about the flattening of distinctions between stars, celebrities and personalities. (Redmond and Holmes 2007: 6)

The Madhuri celebrity text is consolidated through regular appearances at Bollywood concerts and fashion shows, guest spots on television programmes, in advertisements and product endorsements, and via an expanding portfolio of humanitarian and charity work.

'Bollywood entertainment shows' or 'Bollywood concerts', travelling with the Bollywood film industry as it vies for new and non-traditional audiences through initiatives such as the IIFAs (International Indian Film Awards), present film stars, singers and musicians with an entourage of dancers and extras, all appearing in important urban centres across India and the South Asian diaspora. 'These shows comprise of actors singing, dancing, re-enacting favourite film scenes and dialogues, and … promote new film ventures, to packed and excited live audiences' (Dudrah 2012: 77). They showcase 'high production values, aspects of live performance art, pyrotechnics and special effects, and huge stage media assemblages and spectacle that are writ large' (ibid.). As an icon of Bollywood film dance, Madhuri is a popular choice for inclusion in these shows, guest appearing in US cities in the Unforgettable Tour 2008 (featuring among others Amitabh Bachchan and Aishwarya Rai) (ibid.: 82). In 2013, she joined the fourth instalment of Shah Rukh Khan's Temptation Reloaded Tour, which performed a series of concerts in Auckland, Perth, Sydney, and Dubai. Additionally, her dance performances at *Screen*, *Filmfare* and IIFA award shows, as well as younger stars' restaging of her iconic dances as homages, generate considerable excitement and media coverage. As Iyer observes, 'tributes to Dixit's famous dance numbers at the 2010 Filmfare Awards and on reality dance shows such as *Jhalak Dikhhla Jaa* (*Give Us a Glimpse*, Sony India, 2006–11; Colors, 2012–) indicate her pervasive influence on popular Hindi film dance and indeed over Indian popular culture in general' (2015: 130).

The fashion show is another popular and predictable platform where the celebrity presents herself in glamorous, exorbitantly priced designer-marque attire that is exclusively created for her. Madhuri's first ever attendance at a fashion show was for designer Ritu Beri in 1997 during her heyday as the reigning Bollywood star. Since then, she has made numerous appearances at Delhi Fashion Weeks, Manish Malhotra fashion shows, and Save and Empower Girl Child Fashion Show to name just a few instances. She has participated in many magazine fashion photo-sessions as well since she is considered a style icon who had been a trendsetter during her heyday. Film magazines play an important role in connecting stars to consumption, particularly of fashion, with periodicals featuring 'elaborate photo shoots, in which hairstylist, makeup artist, and clothes designer are all credited' or numerous pages devoted to the advertisement of all sorts of products (Wilkinson-Weber 2014: 166).

Guest spots on television programmes ensure that a celebrity maintains her visibility even during a lull in her career, or when she is promoting a forthcoming film or television show. Some notable appearances include those on *Koffee with Karan*, a controversial, high-profile talk show hosted by Bollywood insider, director-producer Karan Johar, in seasons two and three that aired in 2007 and 2011, respectively. She made a solo appearance in season two and in season three she shared the chat show with Sonakshi Sinha. In 2014, Madhuri made her third appearance on *Koffee with Karan*, on its fourth season alongside Juhi Chawla. She has been a guest on *Nach Baliye* (*Let's Dance, Partner*) season one and three, a celebrity-couple dancing competition in 2005 (aired on Star One) and 2007 (aired on Star Plus). Madhuri also appeared on *India's Got Talent* as a guest judge on two separate occasions for the promotion of her last two films *Dedh Ishqiya* and *Gulaab Gang* that were released in early 2014.

Almost every Bollywood actor in the upper echelons of stardom has had some experience working both in film, and in the fashion and advertising business. Brand endorsements and advertising are a crucial measure of the popularity, success, and influence of a celebrity, the quality and quantity of endorsements determining stature in the hierarchy of celebrities. Stars are 'a privileged site for the promulgation and solidification of new consumer ideals' (DeCordova 2001: 108), an 'idol of consumption' (ibid.: 109). Typically, film stars and cricketers in India endorse multiple high-end brands, 'develop[ing] their public persona as a commercial asset and their career choices, in principle [are] devoted to that objective. As the asset appreciates – as the celebrity's fame spreads – so does its earning capacity' (Turner 2007: 193). Edgar Morin reminds us that, 'the star is not only a subject but an object of advertising … . The star is a total item of merchandise: there is not an inch of her body, not a shred of her soul, not a memory of her life that cannot be thrown on the market' for mass consumption (2005: 113). Thus, from anti-ageing cream for the ageing female celebrity, to tea, toothpaste, and rice, Madhuri has thrown her name behind these homely products, consolidating on her dependable, trustworthy homemaker image. As Clare Wilkinson-Weber notes, 'The star's own distinct brand identity, cultivated in films … but tempered in media work outside film, grows as a result of the elaboration of his or her persona through these interconnected realms' (2014: 166). Madhuri is the brand ambassador for Olay Regenerist anti-ageing creams and serum which, along with a balanced diet and

Madhuri's traditional homemaker image evident in endorsements of wholesome foods such as Neesa Basmati rice

exercise, she claims are part of her skincare regime (Paitandy 2011). Her familial, motherly star image is reinforced by other mundane products such as Bush Foods Basmati Rice, Expert Detergent Bar, Comfort Liquid Conditioner, Emami, Oral–B, and Taj Mahal Tea. In 2013 'Dabar India' roped Madhuri in as brand ambassador for Dabur Chyawanprash – endorsing the brand in all campaigns across television, print, and digital media (*Business of Cinema*, October 2013). P. N. Gadgil jewellers signed her as their brand ambassador for two years in 2013 too.

She was lauded by the media for breaking 'the jinx associated with married women in Bollywood, articulately building Brand Madhuri having signed new leading roles, endorsement deals and a successful television stint (sic)' (Srivastava 2013). Her lucrative multi-crore[2] contract to be the brand ambassador of a prominent tea label was reported as the deal that sealed 'her place in the world of endorsement, which is largely ruled by younger faces from Bollywood, the modelling world and sports' (ibid.). The tea advertisement would portray her love for *kathak* and Birju Maharaj could be choreographing the dance. For Josy Paul, chief creative culprit and chairman, BBDO India, Madhuri 'stands the test of time and thus creates authenticity and familiarity for brands. She has eternity written all over her!' (*Midday.com* 15 March 2013). According to famed ad film-maker Prahlad Kakkar,

> The advertisement industry has had a slot for slightly older actresses with grace and mature looks to be presented as the face of certain niche products. Madhuri has smartly handled her career only to emerge as the new face of endorsements. (ibid.)

Thus, the actor brand makes 'for an unusually apt and productive convergence of the interests of manufacturers, advertisers, actors, and – because of the intensification of the effect of star recognizability – film producers' (Wilkinson-Weber 2014: 166).

Over the years, Madhuri has garnered appeal not just as an entertainer but as a genuine humanitarian with an increasingly impressive portfolio of charity work. In 2012, she became a goodwill ambassador and patron for 'Emeralds for Elephants,' a wildlife conservation project for Asian elephants and other endangered species (Forbes). For World Diabetes Day 2013, Madhuri created India's first-ever signature dance step for diabetes to instil solidarity at the launch of Sanofi's 'What Step Will You Take Today?' campaign. Speaking on the occasion, she said her step challenging diabetes was through the way she knew best, dance, which she felt truly united people ('Madhuri Creates First-ever Dance Step for Diabetes' 2013: 3). In 2016, Madhuri was selected as celebrity advocate by the health ministry in collaboration with the United Nations (UN) agency for its flagship pan-Indian MAA (Mother's Absolute Affection) campaign to spread awareness about the benefits of breastfeeding

(Dey 2016: 10). In 2014, she was appointed the brand ambassador for Madhya Pradesh government's 'Mamta Abhiyan', 'a campaign seeking to reduce the maternal and infant mortality rates which are very high in Madhya Pradesh' (*Indian Express*, 7 June 2014). In the same year, Madhuri became UNICEF's 'Celebrity Advocate for Child Rights', making key public-service announcements for child protection, and prevention of child labour and child trafficking, used extensively as inter-personal communication materials for communities across India. As a supporter, she joined a distinguished list of well-known and respected personalities, who serve on behalf of the world's children, bringing 'enormous credibility and energy to the important task of communicating to the broad public (sic) about the importance of child rights and on the vision and values which guide UNICEF's work for children', reiterating that 'every stage in the life cycle of every child is critical and needs [the] utmost attention' (*Indian Express*, 12 June 2014). These humanitarian initiatives have affirmed and solidified Madhuri's clean, wholesome image, while simultaneously promoting her health-conscious, homely, motherly persona.

In 2001, she won Rs. 5,000,000 on *Kaun Banega Crorepati*, a popular game show (India's version of *Who Wants to Be a Millionaire?*), then in its first season on the air. She instructed that her winnings be donated towards the welfare of victims of an earthquake in Gujarat and to an orphanage in Pune. In 2009, she performed for NDTV Toyota Greenathon – India's first-ever nationwide campaign to save the environment and promulgate awareness about environmental issues. NDTV organised India's first twenty-four-hour live telethon, a fundraising event that brings in people to donate money to support TERI's initiative – Lighting a Billion Lives, which aims to provide solar power to villages without electricity. Madhuri became a part of this significant social cause, and she performed her hit numbers on the live show. On 4 February 2012, she interacted with cancer-affected children on World Cancer Day in an event organised by Pawan Hans Helicopters Ltd at Juhu, Mumbai.

Recent films

In a 1996 interview in *Movie*, Madhuri had felt that her 'best [was] yet to come'. She had then opined:

> There is so much more one can do. I don't mean in terms of a hit. I may not have a hit in the future but performance wise, I still feel shackled. I want to break free. There's a lot I am capable of … . (Kalarikal 1996: 56)

Perhaps 'breaking free' was her intention in the second phase of her career when she signed two unconventional projects, *Gulaab Gang* and Abhishek Chaubey's *Dedh Ishqiya* that offered her the rare freedom to delve into hitherto unexplored dimensions of her acting talent, despite her offbeat films, *Gaja Gamini* and *Mrityudand* during her heyday that were dwarfed by her mainstream hits. But, thirty years after she first showed up on screen, Dixit appeared 'keener than ever to shake up the status quo …' (Sen 2014).

In *Gulaab Gang*, Madhuri enacts the feisty role of Rajjo, based loosely on the crusading Uttar Pradesh vigilante Sampat Pal and her brigade of pink-saree-clad women in a village in central India. It focuses on one woman's unequal struggle to empower rural women who have been abused and abandoned, and are considered to have suffered the most oppression at the hands of corrupt politicians and a male chauvinistic society. For Madhuri, it was groundbreaking as she couldn't think of another mainstream Bollywood potboiler that had women in key roles – 'a movie with all the masala, all the dialogue-*baazi*, and yet with a female protagonist and antagonist' (Sen 2014). That a woman was playing that kind of a role was fascinating for her: 'because it changes the rules in one go. It's like throwing down a bowling ball and watching the pins go flying' (ibid.). I read the film as an extension of her character traits and persona in *Mrityudand*, of the avenging, strong woman fighting feudal patriarchal forces. The feminist subtext of female empowerment

Madhuri as the vigilante Rajjo in the feminist film *Gulaab Gang* (2014)

that underpinned her 1990s corpus of films finds overt expression in *Gulaab Gang*. Madhuri felt it spoke about women's rights and education, and society in general and 'was a statement on what's happening around us: laws need to be stronger; we have this whole infrastructure and yet nothing really happens' (ibid.).

Dynamic action sequences of her leaping, bounding, and punching corrupt village men, captured in slow motion and choreographed like balletic dance movements, which she performed without a body double, reveal not just the flexibility, agility, and grace of a seasoned danseuse, but also her training in the martial art of Taekwondo, a little-known fact about her. She and her mother sing the first song after the intermission, 'Rangi Saari Gulaabi,' thereby giving expression to yet another one of her hidden talents. Noted trade analyst and critic Taran Adarsh lauded Madhuri for enacting 'the part of a righteous woman with supreme understanding', commenting that she 'deserves brownie points for a terrific portrayal'. 'In her three-decade-long career, the actress has worked in practically all genres of cinema, but GULAAB GANG [sic] gives her the platform to explore not just the dramatics, but action too' (Gupta 2015: 117).

As Iyer points out, 'these roles are a far cry from those reserved by popular Hindi cinema for older, married actresses in their forties' (2015: 153). While the absence of lead male protagonists (a recent trend in Bollywood new wave) continues to be refreshing, albeit still surprising, there is also the new phenomenon of older female actors starring as lead protagonists. Aside from Madhuri, the popular 1990s actress Juhi Chawla, cast as the antagonist the evil politician Sumitra, are both well past their prime. In the Bombay film industry, while male stars in their fifties romancing twenty year olds is practically the norm, female actors/stars typically have a much shorter shelf life as romantic leads. As discussed earlier, deep-seated ageist biases foreshorten career spans and inhibit character roles for older, thirty-plus, married female stars who are relegated to the unimportant, peripheral characters of mothers, aunts, sisters-in-law, and even grandmothers, but rarely cast as romantic leads.

In this film, however, Madhuri and Chawla are formidable characters endowed with narrative agency and 'strikingly unencumbered by the narrative and representational demands of heterosexual romance' (2015: 153). As Iyer astutely observes,

> [Madhuri's] fame as a dancer-actress produces a different star text than that of her contemporaries like Juhi Chawla or Manisha Koirala, with Dixit's spectacular dancing body proving difficult to fit into the maternal mold reserved for older actresses and resisting declining into character actor oblivion. The kinetic dynamism of Dixit's dancing body (along with her considerable acting prowess of course) allows her to script an entirely new text for the female star in her forties. (ibid.: 152)

Moreover, *Gulaab Gang* is an excellent example of the woman-oriented, feminist films that have become popular with female audiences thronging multiplexes over the past few years. As Adrian Athique and William Hill observe, based on gendered audience sampling in Kolkata multiplexes, there is a significant reemergence of women as a cinema audience, reinforcing the argument 'that this is an important audience demographic who enthusiastically responds to a safer and less male-dominated leisure environment' (2010: 180).

In between her two films, Madhuri breaks more Bollywood rules by performing in an item number (usually reserved for sexy, young female star(lets)) called 'Ghagra' (Skirt) in the blockbuster *Yeh Jawaani Hai Deewani* (*This Youthfulness Is Crazy*). It is delightfully self-reflexive as she makes a grand entrance to the accompanying chants of 'Mohini', evoking memories of her 1988 breakthrough role in *Tezaab*, and flirtatiously matches step with Bollywood royalty and heartthrob, Ranbir Kapoor, junior to her by a mere fifteen years.

Abhishek Chaubey's *Dedh Ishqiya* is a sequel to the unexpectedly popular black comedy *Ishqiya* (*Romance*, 2010) starring Vidya Balan, that continues the progressive trend of older, married, female actors essaying substantive roles in the wake of the success of 'women-centric' new wave cinema ushered in by Balan's *The Dirty Picture* (2011), *Kahaani* (*Story*, 2012), the successful 'comeback' of Sridevi (after a hiatus of fifteen years from the silver screen) with *English Vinglish* (2013), and by Kangana Ranaut's *Queen* (2014). *Dedh Ishqiya* is a decidedly adult, highly nuanced film about conmen posing as Urdu poets who attempt to woo the once-wealthy Begum Para, who are in turn duped by her scheming maid and her. As the deceptive Begum, Madhuri essays one of the few non-Hindu character roles in her illustrious film career; a complex, conflicted character who I see as an extension of the lovelorn Chandramukhi, her critically acclaimed courtesan role in *Devdas*. Birju Maharaj's choreography of 'Hamari Atariya Pe' ('On My Rooftop') is another artistic connection with *Devdas*.

Reflexivity and allusions to Madhuri's stardom and millennial reinvention abound in this delightfully layered portrayal, imbued with a rare delicacy and self-aware grace that is unparalleled in current Hindi cinema. There are extra-textual resonances as the film blurs the real/reel selves – Begum Para/Madhuri's return to the world of classical dance after her marriage forced her to give it up; flashbacks of her younger self who was an accomplished danseuse; elaborate introductions to the Begum's suitors that echo Madhuri's off-screen reality-TV persona, introducing herself to a new generation of young audiences. One of her paramours, the Nawab of Chandpur (portrayed by the legendary character actor Naseeruddin Shah) says, 'I'm an ardent admirer of your dance' and 'Where is the Para of twenty-five years ago?', which have obvious extratextual resonances. The film also gestures towards the ageing celebrity's self-awareness of her marginalised and precarious position in the film industry – the time for being a lover is over for her as she can no longer play the romantic lead. Much like the antiquated world of bankrupt landed aristocracies (*nawabiyat*) and Urdu poetry the Begum inhabits, that is hopelessly out of touch with the rapidly changing world around her, the old norms of Hindi cinema have changed too. 'As things become more "new-age," there's no place for characters with old-world charm, and they try desperately to fit into the new generation', she says (Sen 2014), as Madhuri tries to reconfigure her celebrity text with the help of new media and reality television.

> The film continues the Dixit-as-dance-guru figuration when it concludes with the Begum opening a dance school for young girls, a safe haven for dancing bodies swirling in a homoerotic world of female desire, away from the prying eyes of the male protagonists. (Iyer 2015: 153)

This parallels Madhuri's creation of the online dance academy, DWM.

Unconventional in many ways, *Dedh Ishqiya* is a homoerotic text where same-sex desire is implicit, ambiguous, and nuanced. Centring on a pair of female con artists who are partners/lovers in crime, this is a film where Hindi cinema's most mainstream actress plays a Begum who prefers the company of women and who says she doesn't 'mind being called the new gay icon' (Dedhia 2014). 'We left it to the viewer to interpret it themselves: it could be two women who were fed up of the men in their lives and they want to be by themselves, or it could be something else' (Sen 2014). Madhuri believes that women are now getting more textured roles. Begum Para is a fully developed character, not the usual clichéd, stereotyped, one-dimensional female character that commercial Hindi cinema has been infamous for. And the film is 'not just a revenge drama, and she's not either avenger or victim, which is what heroine-oriented films used to mean' (Sen 2014). Madhuri is also gratified that female characters no longer need to justify their ambitions. It is refreshingly devoid of moralising and contrived justifications for the actions and (same-sex) desire of these two women protagonists, which is a significant departure from the typical Hindi film. Anupama Chopra's review for *Hindustan Times* lauds 'the film [for] giv[ing] us women who are unapologetically scheming and lusty. They break all the rules and get away with it. It's wonderfully refreshing … Madhuri is still compelling' (2014).

Although her transmedia celebrity work and recent films are steps in the right direction, I believe that Madhuri's potential remains untapped and her best film is yet to come. In 1997, *Screen* magazine had written:

> Now is the time for Madhuri to do something memorable, something which will be remembered for as long as Indian cinema is remembered … . Now is the time for Madhuri to know that her true worth, her true potential has not been realised yet. ('Now's the Time, Ms Dixit' 1997: 32)

Twenty years later, it is still applicable for the consolidation of the Madhuri celebrity text as she ventures into regional cinema with her debut Marathi film, *Bucket List* (2018).

NOTES

Introduction

1 Madhuri Dixit deploys this binary of *filmi* vs middle class consistently throughout her career to great advantage. *Filmi* is 'an Indian English term used pejoratively to describe behavior, fashion, and lifestyles that appear to be overly influenced by, or evocative of, popular Hindi cinema or the film industry. *Filmi* also implies ostentation, flamboyance, crudeness, immorality or amorality, and a disregard for formal education.' Middle class denotes 'a social or behavioral norm that is *filmi*'s opposite, marked by modesty, thrift, propriety, morality, and a value for education' (Ganti 2011: 142).

2 See S. Kakar, '"Starring" Madhuri as Durga: The Madhuri Dixit Temple and Performative Fan-Bhakti of Pappu Sardar', *International Journal of Hindu Studies* vol. 13 no. 3 (2009), pp. 391–416.

3 The cinematic figuration of the Indian female body has been traditionally contentious, often conflated with notions of national/communal/religious honour or *izzat*. In order to manage these anxieties, the representation of the female star in popular Hindi cinema, from the 1950s through the 1980s, was neatly split between the virginal heroine, and the morally dubious, publicly performing, Westernised vamp. These stereotypical characters embodied moral binaries of tradition/modernity, East/West, wife/whore, and were identified by overt signifiers such as their names, locations, occupations, costuming, and dance movements employed in

song picturisations, the heroine displaying coyness while her scantily clad counterpart indulged in uninhibited, raunchy cabaret dances usually performed at nightclubs and bars. For further discussions on the heroine and vamp representations, see Ranjani Mazumdar, *Bombay Cinema: An Archive of the City* (Delhi: Permanent Black, 2007); Asha Kasbekar, 'Hidden Pleasures: Negotiating the Myth of the Female Ideal in Popular Hindi Cinema', in R. Dwyer and C. Pinney (eds), *Pleasure and the Nation* (New Delhi: Oxford University Press, 2001), pp. 286–308; Jerry Pinto, *Helen: The Life and Times of an H-Bomb* (New Delhi: Penguin, 2006); and Anustup Basu (2013: 139–57) on Helen.

Chapter 1

1 '*Screen India* was the most powerful industry publication through the 1970s and 1980s; for a considerable part of this time, its third-page advertisement was the hottest real estate in Hindi film publicity, reserved largely for paid announcements for films celebrating a grand theatrical run, or first posters for films with whopping budgets. It was, therefore, rather startling to see a dramatic six-page ad starting on page three "launching" a heroine who wasn't merely unknown, but unknown because her first five films had flopped' (Sen 2014). Madhuri recalls: 'I remember the first time I saw my name in print was in *Screen*. It was my first major ad campaign, yes, the six-page campaign that introduced me. It was Mr Subhash Ghai's idea' ('Madhuri Dixit: "They're Too Precious"' 1997: 4).

2 *Film Information*, 26 September 1987.
Full page promotional advertisement in the leading trade paper proclaiming:

> "So we were right …
> Clouds have gone/A Star is Born … /And her name is … /Madhuri Dixit/Today, there is one voice all around … /Whether it is North or South –/Madhuri is THE Star!/Just wait and watch her in our UTTAR DAKSHIN."

3 The hero who suits Madhuri best is ... 53 per cent voted for Anil Kapoor (*Movie* March 1996: 50).

4 'Good families are defined by their upper-caste status, middle-class to upper-class position, high levels of formal education, practice of modern professional occupations (medicine, engineering, law, journalism, civil service, teaching), and gendered norms of sexual modesty' (Ganti 2012: 121).

5 In a more recent interview on the release of the critically acclaimed, feminist film *Pink* (2016), Amitabh Bachchan confirms that in his hey day the only woman present on film sets apart from the actress was her mother (Mukherjee 2016: 12).

6 Elucidating upon the key differences among these star elements, Neepa Majumdar points out that 'gossip, rumor, and scandal belong in a shared network of rhetorical forms of public discourse, but can be usefully distinguished from one another. While gossip usually pertains to knowledge about private or other aspects of personal lives that are not meant to be publicly available and are coded as privileged information, scandal is, by definition, knowledge of a public nature ... . Unlike scandal, however, gossip and rumor function rhetorically in a field of uncertainty, lacking accuracy and with no source capable of verification' (2009: 39). Furthermore, as Paul McDonald insightfully suggests, 'while scandal can split a star's private life into two, rumor and gossip can divide audiences into two groups: those "in-the-know" and everyone else' (Shingler 2012: 145).

Chapter 2

1 VCRs were expensive items that only affluent upper-middle-class families could afford. I recall my mother had purchased a BPL Sanyo multisystem video player (VCP) that cost a whopping Rs. 13,000 in 1992.

2 For political and historical studies of Indian television, see, among others, Nilanjana Gupta, *Switching Channels: Ideologies of Television in India* (1998); Melissa Butcher, *Transnational Television, Cultural Identity, and*

Change: When Stars Came to India (2003); and Shanti Kumar, *Gandhi Meets Primetime: Globalization and Nationalism in Indian Television* (2006).

3 See Arvind Rajagopal's *Politics after Television: Hindu Nationalism and the Reshaping of the Public in India* (New Delhi: Cambridge University Press, 2001) for a fascinating examination of the imbrication of Hindu nationalist politics with 1980s Indian television programming.

4 The Hindu Right is a nationalist, right-wing political entity devoted to creating a Hindu state in India. It includes the Bharatiya Janata Party (BJP) (the political arm of the Right, which was in power from 1999 to 2004 and was defeated by the Congress in the 2004 general elections), the Rashtriya Swayam Sevak (RSS) (the main ideological component of the Right), and the Vishwa Hindu Parishad (VHP). Other parties include the extremist, anti-Muslim regional party Shiv Sena. These organisations collectively promote the ideology of Hindutva – an ideology that seeks to establish a Hindu state in India. There are several offshoots and newer segments of the Hindu Right, which include the Bajrang Dal (BJD) and women's wings of the main and subsidiary bodies. Together they are the Sangh Parivar, or the United Family. For critical accounts of the rise of Hindutva, see, among others, Tapan Basu *et al.*, *Khaki Shorts and Saffron Flags* (1993); Thomas Hansen, *The Saffron Wave: Democracy and Hindu Nationalism in Modern India* (2001); Christopher Jaffrelot, *The Hindu Nationalist Movement in India* (1996).

Chapter 3

1 Here I follow the definition of performance advanced by Richard Dyer: 'Predominantly performance has been concerned with the creation … and presentation of character' (1998: 132).

> Performance is what the performer does in addition to the actions/functions s/he performs in the plot and the lines s/he is given to say. Performance is how the action/function is done, how the lines are said. The signs of performance are: facial expression; voice, gestures

(principally of hands and arms, but also of any limb, e.g. neck, leg); body posture (how someone is standing or sitting); body movement (movement of the whole body, including how someone stands up or sits down, how they walk, run, etc.). (ibid.: 134)

2 Madhuri Dixit quoted in Anon, 'How Success Has Changed Madhuri Dixit,' *Star & Style* 21 March–6 April 1991, p. 17.

3 This is evident from two photographs displayed at Saroj Khan's Dance Academy in Goregaon, Mumbai – one is of Madhuri being taught by Khan to arch her back and to hold that dancing position, and the other shows Khan teaching her to perfect a 'mudra'/hand gesture.

4 Anecdotal evidence gleaned from my interviews with industry personnel confirm Saroj Khan's reputation as a perfectionist and hard taskmaster: long and arduous practice sessions and rehearsals were devoted to perfecting minute details such as trying to perfect the angle of the feet of a group of background dancers accompanying Madhuri that were ever so slightly out of step (personal interview with Soumik Sen, 1 July 2013 in Mumbai).

5 A March 1998 *Movie* magazine poll question 'Who is the best dancer amongst today's heroines?' revealed that Madhuri was clearly ahead with 52 per cent votes, while her rival, Karisma received 40 per cent ('Movie Poll,' March 1998: 72).

6 Director Ketan Mehta quoted in Jain 1990.

7 For an insightful analysis of the censorship debates and protracted legal controversy surrounding this song and the film, see Monika Mehta, 'Tracking the Twists and Turns in the *Khalnayak* Debates on Censorship' in *Censorship and Sexuality in Bombay Cinema* (Austin: University of Texas Press, 2011).

8 Sumita Chakravarty's book *National Identity in Indian Popular Cinema, 1947–1987* (Austin: University of Texas Press, 1993) provides an insightful analysis on masquerade and masculinity.

9 Queer, transgressive undertones may be discerned in a few of Madhuri's iconic song picturisations, subsumed within seemingly rigid heteronormative texts: first, the 'Choli ke Peeche Kya Hai' number is sung between two women, and the cinematography and editing

employed, through a relay of point-of-view shots exchanged between these women, can lend itself to a queer interpretation; second, in an otherwise conservative, heteronormative, bourgeois text, *HAHK*, produced when the Hindutva movement was ominously gaining momentum, there is the unexpected transgressive, queer space of the song sequence 'Didi Tera Devar Deewana' where one of the minor female characters indulges in cross-dressing. Decades later, the queer subtext to the Madhuri phenomenon is given fuller expression in the role of a retired danseuse in *Dedh Ishqiya* and I contend that it is not a coincidence.

10 'In this use and focus of songs as erotic, Hindi cinema draws on, and indeed continues, the ancient tradition of public female performance in India as seduction and erotic entertainment dating back to courtesans and "nautch girls" as well as more modern phenomena such as cabaret, which was popular in Bombay and many other smaller towns of India in the mid-twentieth century' (Morcom 2011: 168).

Chapter 4

1 All episodes of *So You Think You Can Dance – Ab India Ki Baari* can be viewed on the following website: http://www.ozee.com/shows/so-you-think-you-can-dance.

2 Crore is an Indian term denoting ten million.

BIBLIOGRAPHY

Ali, 'Sweetness and Light', *Screen* 29 May 1986, p. 6.

Anon, '*Abodh*: Insipidly Recycled Romance', *Screen* 21 September 1984, p. 4.

Anon, 'About Us', Dance with Madhuri (DWM), <http://www.dancewithmadhuri.com/misc/#!/misc/footer/aboutDWM> (accessed 30 December 2016).

Anon, 'Anil Kapoor: "They Are Jealous!"', *Filmfare* July 1990, p. 20.

Anon, 'Best Actress Madhuri Dixit Dil to Pagal Hai', *Filmfare* March 1998, p. 44.

Anon, 'Best Film–Yash Chopra: DTPH', *Filmfare* March 1998, p. 58.

Anon, 'Filmfare's 50 Most Beautiful People: Madhuri Dixit', *Filmfare* 11 November 2009, p. 101.

Anon, *Film Information* 21 November 1987.

Anon, 'Has Sanjay Changed Madhuri?', *Showtime* March 1993, pp. 8–9, 11–14.

Anon, 'Heart to Heart', *Screen* 30 April 1993, p. 25.

Anon, 'Heartbreaks …', *Movie* July 1989, pp. 27–8.

Anon, 'How Success Has Changed Madhuri Dixit', *Star & Style* 21 March–6 April 1991, pp. 17–19.

Anon, 'Husain on Madhuri's Marriage!', *Cine Blitz* December 1999, pp. 74–80.

Anon, 'Indra Kumar: They Said I Was Crazy to Sign Aamir!', *Filmfare* August 1990, p. 48.

Anon, 'Madhuri-Ash Clash! Sanjay's Revenge?', *Cine Blitz* August 2002, pp. 52–4.

Anon, 'Madhuri Brand Ambassador of MP Scheme', *Indian Express* 7 June 2014, <http://indianexpress.com/article/india/india-others/madhuri-brand-ambassador-of-mp-scheme/> (accessed 30 December 2016).

Anon, 'Madhuri Creates First-Ever Dance Step for Diabetes', *Calcutta Times, Times of India* 14 November 2013, p. 3.

Anon, 'Madhuri Dixit', *Forbes India*, <http://www.forbesindia.com/profile/madhuri-dixit/1395/78> (accessed 22 December 2016).

Anon, 'Madhuri Dixit Joins Hands with UNICEF', *Indian Express* 12 June 2014, <http://indianexpress.com/article/entertainment/bollywood/madhuri-dixit-joins-hands-with-unicef/> (accessed 22 December 2016).

Anon, 'Madhuri Dixit: One-Up!', *Filmfare* February 1995, pp. 30–5.

Anon, 'Madhuri Dixit Named Most Inspirational Female Bollywood Icon', *Hindustan Times* 2 April 2014, <http://www.hindustantimes.com/entertainment/bollywood/madhuri-dixit-named-most-inspirational-female-bollywood-icon/article1-1203367.aspx> (accessed 22 December 2016).

Anon, 'Madhuri Dixit: Special Award on Completion of 25 Years in Hindi Cinema', *Filmfare* 16 March 2011, p. 133.

Anon, 'Madhuri Dixit's Shocking New Lifestyle!!!', *Stardust* March 1988, pp. 90–5.

Anon, 'Madhuri Dixit: "They're Too Precious",' *Screen* 10 January 1997, p. 4.

Anon, 'Madhuri Dixit's Wax Statue Unveiled at Madame Tussauds', *Indian Express* 7 March 2012, <http://indianexpress.com/article/entertainment/entertainment-others/madhuri-dixits-wax-statue-unveiled-at-madame-tussauds/> (accessed 22 December 2016).

Anon, 'Madhuri Dixit Signs a Multi-crore Deal with a Tea Brand', *Midday.com*, 15 March 2013, <movies.ndtv.com/Bollywood> (accessed 16 December 2016).

Anon, 'Madhuri Dixit: The Endorsement Diva', *Business of Cinema* News Network, 31 October 2013, <http://businessofcinema.com/news/madhuri-dixit-endorsement-diva/115579> (accessed 16 December 2016).

Anon, 'Madhuri's Personal Notes on Mr Right', *Showtime* November 1993, pp. 21–4.

Anon, 'Madhuri Returns to TV after Two Years as Judge for Reality Show Dance Deewane', *First Post*, 24 April 2018. <https://www.firstpost.com/entertainment/madhuri-dixit-returns-to-tv-after-two-years-as-judge-for-reality-show-dance-deewane-4443571.html> (accessed 8 August 2018).

Anon, 'Now's the Time, Ms Dixit', *Screen* 19 December 1997, p. 32.

Anon, 'Revealed: Why Madhuri Ditched Jhalak for So You Think You Can Dance', *T2 Online Entertainment* 20 April 2016, <http://t2online.com/entertainment/revealed-why-madhuri-ditched-jhalak-for-so-you-think-you-can-dance/cid/1.38128> (accessed 30 December 2016).

Anon, 'The "Kiss MS"!', *Filmfare* April 1990, p. 82.

Anon, *Filmfare* 25 January 1990, p. 58.

Anon, *Filmfare* April 1995, p. 41.

Anon, 'Movie Poll', *Movie* March 1995, p. 40.

Anon, 'Movie Poll', *Movie* March 1998, p. 72.

Anon, "My Fashion Label Resonates With Me: Madhuri Dixit." *Business Standard*. 31 July, 2015. <https://www.business-standard.com/article/news-ians/my-fashion-label-resonates-with-me-madhuri-dixit-115073100545_1.html> (accessed 8 August 2018).

Anon, *Screen* 14 December 1990, p. 26.

Anon, *Screen* 8 February 1991.

Anon, *Screen* 17 May 1991, p. 2.

Anon, 'Star in Her Name', *Calcutta Times, Times of India* 19 June 2012, p. 1.

Anon, *Star & Style* 6–19 November 1987, p. 24.

Anon, *Star & Style* 26 February–10 March 1988a, pp. 55–7.

Anon, *Star & Style* 18 November–1 December 1988b, pp. 67–9.

Anon, *Stardust* February 1990, pp. 64–9.

Anon, 'Suicide Bent?', *Filmfare* August 1990, p. 8.

Anon, 'Why Madhuri Lost Barjatya's Film!', *Cine Blitz* 16 January 1998, pp. 36–8.

Alberoni, F., 'The Powerless "Elite": Theory and Sociological Research on the Phenomenon of the Stars', in S. Redmond and S. Holmes (eds), *Stardom and Celebrity: A Reader* (Los Angeles, CA and London: Sage Publications, 2007), pp. 65–77.

Arora, N., 'Madhuri Dixit: Simple, Graceful, Controlled, Elusive!', *Showtime* July 1989.

Athique, A. and Hill, D., *The Multiplex in India: A Cultural Economy of Urban Leisure* (London and New York: Routledge, 2010).

Awaasthi, K., 'Dance Isn't Work for Me, I Have Fun Doing It: Madhuri Dixit', *Hindustan Times* 5 June 2014, p. 6.

Bamzai, K., *Madhuri Dixit – A Woman of Her Times* (New Delhi: Zubaan, 2008).

Banaji, S., *Reading 'Bollywood': The Young Audience and Hindi Films* (Basingstoke: Palgrave Macmillan, 2012).

Basu, A., *Bollywood in the Age of New Media: The Geo-Televisual Aesthetic* (Edinburgh: Edinburgh University Press, 2012).

Basu, A., '"The Face That Launched a Thousand Ships": Helen and Public Femininity in Hindi Film', in M. Sen and A. Basu (eds), *Figurations in Indian Film* (Basingstoke: Palgrave Macmillan, 2013), pp. 139–57.

Benjamin, W., 'The Work of Art in the Age of Mechanical Reproduction', in S. Redmond and S. Holmes (eds), *Stardom and Celebrity: A Reader* (Los Angeles, CA and London: Sage Publications, 2007), pp. 25–33.

Bharadwaj, P., 'Madhuri Dixit: No Guts, No Glory', *Filmfare* September 1994, pp. 50–2.

Bharadwaj, P., 'The Big Price Rise', *Filmfare* October 1995, pp. 21–4.

Bharucha, R., 'Utopia in Bollywood: *HAHK ...!*', *Economic and Political Weekly* 15 April 1995, p. 804.

Bhatia, S., *Amar Akbar Anthony: Masala, Madness and Manmohan Desai* (Noida: HarperCollins India, 2013).

Bhattacharjya, N. and Mehta, M., 'From Bombay to Bollywood: Tracking Cinematic and Musical Tours', in S. Gopal and S. Moorti (eds), *Global Bollywood: Travels of Hindi Song and Dance* (Minneapolis and London: University of Minnesota Press, 2008), pp. 105–31.

Bhaumik, K., 'Sulochana: Clothes, Stardom and Gender in Early Indian Cinema', in R. Moseley (ed.), *Fashioning Film Stars: Dress, Culture, Identity* (New York: Routledge, 2005), pp. 87–97.

Biswas, P., 'Dixit Deep Down Inside!', *Cine Blitz International* February 1992.

Bose, N., 'The Hindu Right and the Politics of Censorship: Three Case Studies of Policing Hindi Cinema, 1992–2002', *The Velvet Light Trap: A Critical Journal of Film and Television* vol. 63 (2009), pp. 22–33.

Bose, N., 'Between the Godfather and the Mafia: Situating Right-Wing Interventions in the Bombay Film Industry (1992–2002)', *Studies in South Asian Film and Media* vol. 1 no. 1 (2009), pp. 23–43.

Bose, N., 'The Central Board of Film Certification Correspondence Files (1992–2002): A Discursive Rhetoric of Moral Panic, "Public" Protest and Political Pressure', *Cinema Journal* vol. 49 no. 3 (2010), pp. 67–87.

Bose, N., 'From Superman to *Shahenshah*: Stardom and the Transnational Corporeality of Hrithik Roshan', in M. Sen and A. Basu (eds), *Figurations in Indian Film* (Basingstoke: Palgrave Macmillan, 2013), pp. 158–78.

Bose, N. '"Bollywood's Fourth Khan": Deconstructing the "Hatke" Stardom of Vidya Balan in Popular Hindi Cinema', *Celebrity Studies* vol. 5 no. 4 (2014), pp. 394–409.

Chakravarty, S., *National Identity in Indian Popular Cinema, 1947–1987* (Austin: University of Texas Press, 1993).

Chatterjee, P., *The Nation and Its Fragments: Colonial and Postcolonial Histories* (Princeton, NJ: Princeton University Press, 2003).

Chopra, A., 'Madhuri Magic', in *First Day First Show: Writing from the Bollywood Trenches* (New Delhi: Penguin India, 2011), pp. 38–47.

Chopra, A., 'The Comeback Girls', *Open Magazine* 20 August 2011b, <http://www.openthemagazine.com/article/voices/the-comeback-girls#.TnjVnK8Egbk.email> (accessed 30 December 2016).

Chopra, A., 'Movie Review: Many Things to Enjoy in Dedh Ishqiya, Writes Anupama Chopra', *Hindustan Times* 11 January 2014, <http://www.hindustantimes.com/movie-reviews/movie-review-many-things-to-enjoy-in-dedh-ishqiya-writes-anupama-chopra/story-QRicJrYAWCArn5Drh9o8MJ.html> (accessed 2 November 2016).

deCordova, R., *Picture Personalities: The Emergence of the Star System in America* (Urbana and Chicago: University of Illinois Press, 2001).

Dedhia, S., 'Madhuri Dixit: "I Don't Mind Being Called the New Gay Icon"', *Rediff.com* 20 February 2014, <http://www.rediff.com/movies/slide-show/slide-show-1-madhuri-dixit-i-dont-mind-being-called-the-new-gay-icon/20140220.htm> (accessed 2 November 2016).

Dey, S., 'Mom's Milk Can Prevent 20% Infant Deaths', *Times of India* 9 August 2016, p. 10.

Divecha, K., 'Looking Back in Anger! Madhuri Blasts Her Detractors!', *Showtime* March 1991.

D'Souza, A., 'Yesterday Once More', *Cine Blitz* May 2006, pp. 92–6.

Dudrah, R., *Bollywood Travels: Culture, Diaspora and Border Crossings in Popular Hindi Cinema* (Abingdon and New York: Routledge, 2012).

Dwyer, R., 'Bombay Ishtyle', in S. Bruzzi and P. C. Gibson (eds), *Fashion Cultures: Theories, Explorations and Analysis* (London and New York: Routledge, 2000), pp. 178–90.

Dyer, R., *Heavenly Bodies:Film Stars and Society*, Basingstoke: Macmillan, 1986. First Edition.

Dyer, R., *Heavenly Bodies: Film Stars and Society* (London: BFI, 1987).

Dyer, R., *Stars* (London: BFI, 1998).

Dyer, R., 'Heavenly Bodies', in S. Redmond and S. Holmes (eds), *Stardom and Celebrity: A Reader* (Los Angeles, CA and London: Sage Publications, 2007), pp. 85–9.

Elley, D., 'Film Reviews: *Devdas*', *Variety* 17–23 June 2002, pp. 24–5.

Ellis, J., 'Stars as Cinematic Phenomenon', in J. G. Butler (ed), *Star Texts, Image and Performance in Film and Television* (Detroit, MI: Wayne State University Press, 1991), pp. 300–15.

Farook, F., 'Life Is Beautiful', *Filmfare* 13 April 2011.

Gandhy, B. and Thomas, R., 'Three Indian Film Stars', in C. Gledhill (ed.), *Stardom: Industry of Desires* (London and New York: Routledge, 1991), pp. 107–31.

Ganti, T., 'Mumbai versus Bollywood: The Hindi Film Industry and the Politics of Cultural Heritage in Contemporary India', in A. P. Kavoori and A. Punathambekar (eds), *Global Bollywood* (New York and London: New York University Press, 2008), pp. 52–78.

Ganti, T., *Producing Bollywood: Inside the Contemporary Hindi Film Industry* (Durham, NC and London: Duke University Press, 2011).

Garimella, S., 'After Madhuri Who', *Movie* September 1995, pp. 24–8.

Ghai, S., 'She's the Best after Sridevi', *Filmfare* 10 October 1988, n.p.

Ghosh, S., 'The Importance of Being Madhuri Dixit', *Zee Premiere* 2000, pp. 164–9.

Gledhill, C., *Stardom: Industry of Desires* (London and New York: Routledge, 1991).

Goldenberg, S., 'Heartbreak for Millions as Indian Film Idol Weds', *Guardian* 8 November 1999, <https://www.theguardian.com/world/1999/nov/08/bollywood.film> (accessed 22 December 2016).

Gopal, S. and Sen, B., 'Inside and Out: Song and Dance in Bollywood Cinema', in R. Dudrah and J. Desai (eds), *The Bollywood Reader* (Maidenhead: Open University Press, 2008), pp. 146–57.

Gopal, S., *Conjugations: Marriage and Form in New Bollywood Cinema* (Chicago, IL: University of Chicago Press, 2011).

Gopalan, L., *Cinema of Interruptions: Action Genres in Contemporary Indian Cinema* (London: BFI, 2002).

Gupta, S., '*Kahaani, Gulaab Gang* and *Queen*: Remaking the Queens of Bollywood', *South Asian Popular Culture* vol. 13 no. 2 (2015), pp. 107–23, DOI:10.1080/14746689.2015.1087107.

Hansen, M. B., *New Philosophy for New Media* (Cambridge, MA: MIT Press, 2005).

Hedge, M., '1986 – The Tilting Merry-Go-Round', *Star & Style* 19 December–1 January 1987, p. 9.

Hegde, R., 'Madhuri Dixit: "I Haven't Really Been in Shape"', *Rediff.com* 15 December 2010.

Iyer, B., 'Diva (stating) Dixit: Pausing at the Crossing', *Showtime* 30 November 1998, pp. 18–24.

Iyer, M., 'How Kushboo Lost the Man to Madhuri', *Star and Style* 23 May–5 June 1986, pp. 31–3, 45.

Iyer, U., 'Stardom Ke Peeche Kya Hai?/What Is behind the Stardom? Madhuri Dixit, the Production Number, and the Construction of the Female Star Text in 1990s Hindi Cinema', *Camera Obscura* 90 vol. 30 no. 3 (2015), pp. 128–59.

Jagirdhar-Saxena, S., 'Flashdance', *Filmfare* 1 June 1989.

Jain, M., 'The 80s Cinema: Triumph Trauma and Tears', *India Today* 15 January 1990, pp. 44–9.

John, A. P., 'His Ambition Changes Lives', *Screen* 30 April 1993a, pp. 21, 27.

John, A. P., 'She's Fate's Favourite Woman, Too', *Screen* 17 September 1993b, p. 21.

Juluri, V., 'Global Weds Local: The Reception of *Hum Aapke Hain Kaun*', *European Journal of Cultural Studies* vol. 2 no. 2 (1999), pp. 231–48.

Kalarikal, A., 'Eight–Stounding', *Movie* February 1996, pp. 48–56.

Karmalkar, D., 'Shiamak Davar: I Want to Dance with Madhuri', *Screen* 22 May 1998, p. 13.

Kasbekar, A., 'Hidden Pleasures: Negotiating the Myth of the Female Ideal in Popular Hindi Cinema', in C. Pinney and R. Dwyer (eds), *Pleasure and the Nation: The History, Politics and Consumption of Public Culture in India* (New Delhi and Oxford: Oxford University Press, 2003), pp. 286–308.

Kaur, R., and Mazzarella, W., (eds) *Censorship in South Asia: Cultural Regulation from Sedition to Seduction* (Bloomington: Indiana University Press, 2009).

Kazmi, F., *The politics of India's conventional cinema: Imaging a universe, subverting a multiverse* (New Delhi: Sage Publications, 1999).

Kazmi, N., *The Dream Merchants of Bollywood* (New Delhi: UBSPD, 1998).

Kothari, J., 'Sanjay Dutt or Superstardom! Madhuri's Choice', *Movie* August 1993.

Kothari, J., 'Madhur(i) Superior: "I Haven't Made Any Friends Here"', *Movie* October 1994, pp. 30–4.

Kothari, J., 'Into the Mind of Madhuri', *Movie* June 1995, pp. 24–9, 94.

Kothari, J., 'Can Madhuri Dixit Wear a New Face?', *Movie* May 1998, pp. 16–20.

Kulkarni, S., 'Alice Doesn't Live Here Anymore!', *Cine Blitz* January 2008, pp. 80–6.

Majumdar, N., *Wanted Cultured Ladies Only: Female Stardom and Cinema in India, 1930s to 1950s* (Urbana-Champaign: University of Illinois Press, 2009).

Masand, R., 'Gautam Rajadhyaksha: Shooting from the Lip', *Screen* 22 August 1997, p. 16.

Mathai Singh, M., 'Ek Do Teen & Loads More', *Cine Blitz* July 1989, pp. 52–9.

Mazumdar, R., *Bombay Cinema: An Archive of the City* (Delhi: Permanent Black, 2007).

McDonald, P., *The Star System: Hollywood's Production of Popular Identities* (London: Wallflower Press, 2000).

Meeuf, R. and Raphael, R., *Transnational Stardom: International Celebrity in Film and Popular Culture* (New York: Palgrave Macmillan, 2013).

Mehta, M., *Censorship and Sexuality in Bombay Cinema* (Austin: University of Texas Press, 2011).

Mehrotra, P.K., 'How We Got Aamir, Madhuri Home', *Sunday Times of India* 31 July 2016, p. 14.

Mitra, A., 'Bollyweb: Search for Bollywood on the Web and See What Happens!', in A. P. Kavoori and A. Punathambekar (eds), *Global Bollywood* (New York and London: New York University Press, 2008), pp. 268–81.

Mohamed, K., 'I Wanted to Be a Nun', *Filmfare* October 1992, pp. 6–11.

Mohamed, K., 'Madhuri Dixit: 1994 Her Love Story', *Filmfare* November 1994, pp. 54–60.

Mohamed, K., 'Madhuri Dixit: Fame Fatale', March 1997, pp. 59–68.

Mohamed, K., 'Internal Affairs: A Passion Play with Madhuri Dixit', *Filmfare* February 1998, pp. 26–34.

Morcom, A., 'Tapping the Mass Market: The Commercial Life of Hindi Film Songs', in S. Gopal and S. Moorti (eds), *Global Bollywood: Travels of Hindi Song and Dance* (Minneapolis and London: University of Minnesota Press, 2008), pp. 63–84.

Morcom, A., 'Film Songs and the Cultural Synergies of Bollywood in and Beyond South Asia', in R. Dwyer and J. Pinto (eds), *Beyond the Boundaries of Bollywood: The Many Forms of Hindi Cinema* (New Delhi: Oxford University Press, 2011), pp. 156–87.

Morin, E., *The Stars*, trans. Richard Howard (Minneapolis and London: University of Minnesota Press, 2005).

Mukherjee, M., 'The Younger Generation Is Far More Accomplished than I Am', *Calcutta Times* 17 September 2016, p. 12.

Mukherjee, R., 'Sound and Fury', *Filmfare* October 1990, pp. 28–35.

Nilesh, P., 'High on Heroines', *Filmfare* May 1996, pp. 28–31.

Nivas, N., 'Colour Me Purple, *Indian Express* 2 November 2012, <http://archive.indianexpress.com/news/colour-me-purple-/1025169> (accessed 13 November 2016).

Paitandy, P., 'The Madhuri Magic', *Hindu*, 3 November 2011, <http://www.thehindu.com/features/metroplus/the-madhuri-magic/article2594662.

ece?homepage=true#.TrMTCFCM-yc.email> (accessed 13 December 2016).

Pammi, S., *Cine Blitz* May 1999a, pp. 48–51.

Pammi, S., 'With Each New Woman I Learn a New Line: Ghai', *Cine Blitz* September 1999b, pp. 36–40.

Pillai, J., 'Mission: Possible', *Filmfare* October 1996, pp. 44–9.

Pillai, J., 'Let's Get Real', *Filmfare* July 1997, p. 51.

Pillai, J., 'The Men Attraction: On the Hot Seat with Madhuri Dixit', *Filmfare* January 1999, pp. 24–8.

Pillai, J., 'Ms Sunshine', *Filmfare* June 2007, pp. 56–60.

Pradhan, B. S., 'I'm Not Involved with Sanjay Dutt', *Showtime* May 1993, pp. 10–14.

Pradhan, B. S., 'Either Way I'm Getting Divorced! Madhuri Has the Last Laugh', *Movie* June 2002, pp. 52–7.

Pradhan, B. S., 'Love in Times of Terror', *Telegraph* 29 May 2011. <http://www.telegraphindia.com/1110529/jsp/7days/story_14043651.jsp> (accessed 18 December 2016).

Prasad, M., *Ideology of the Hindi Film: A Historical Construction* (Delhi: Oxford University Press, 1998).

Prasad, M., *Cine-Politics: Film Stars and Political Existence in South India* (New Delhi: Orient Blackswan, 2014).

Punathambekar, A., *From Bombay to Bollywood: The Making of a Global Media Industry* (New York: New York University Press, 2013).

Rajadhyaksha, A., 'The Bollywoodization of the Indian Cinema: Cultural Nationalism in a Global Arena', in A. Kavoori and A. Punathambekar (eds), *Global Bollywood* (New York and London: New York University Press, 2008), pp. 17–40.

Rajadhyaksha, A. and Willemen, P., 'Madhuri Dixit', in *Encyclopaedia of Indian Cinema* (London: Routledge, 1999).

Rajadhyaksha, G., *Faces: A Collection of Indian Film Personality Portraits. Cine Blitz* Presentation (Dubai: Dolphin Media Group, 1997).

Rane, P., 'Mad about Madhuri', *Savvy* October 2010, pp. 16–33.

Rao, M., 'Dil to Pagal Hai: All About Loving and Losing, Loving and Winning', *Screen* 14 November 1997, p. 10.

Redmond, S. and Holmes, S. (eds), *Stardom and Celebrity: A Reader* (Los Angeles, CA and London: Sage Publications, 2007), pp. 1–11.

Reddy, S., 'The 'Kiss MS!', *Filmfare* April 1990, p. 82.

Rege, P., 'Million Dollar Mom', *India Today* 10 January 2013, <http://indiatoday.intoday.in/story/million-dollar-mom/1/241632.html> (accessed 24 November 2016).

Sanjay, K. S., 'The New Sensation', *Filmfare* 16–30 April 1986, p. 8.

Sanjay, K. S., 'Madhuri Wins (Un)Popularity Poll!', *Star & Style* 9–22 September 1988, pp. 23–5.

Sawant, P., 'I've Never Revelled in My Stardom', *Times Life!* Sunday Times of India Supplement 15 September 2013, p. 1.

Shahani, R., 'M. F. Husain–Madhuri Dixit: Art for Heart's Sake', *Filmfare* July 1995, pp. 32–8.

Sharma, G., 'I Enjoy the Peace after the Show-Sha', *Times of India* 23 July 2014, p. 4.

Shingler, M., *Star Studies: A Critical Guide* (London: BFI, 2012).

Shresthova, S., 'Dancing to an Indian Beat: "Dola" Goes My Diasporic Heart', in S. Gopal and S. Moorti (eds), *Global Bollywood: Travels of Hindi Song and Dance* (Minneapolis and London: University of Minnesota Press, 2008), pp. 250–3.

Sen, R., 'Queen: What Madhuri Dixit did next', *The Caravan–A Journal of Politics and Culture* 1 June 2014, <http://caravanmagazine.in> (accessed 30 December 2016).

Singh, M. M., 'Ek Do Teen & Loads More', *Cine Blitz* July 1989, p. 57.

Singh, S., 'An Ode to Beauty', *Hello!* June 2014, pp. 66–77.

Sinha, S., 'The Publicity Game!', *Times Life!* Sunday Times of India Supplement 10 April 2011, p. 1.

Sircar, A., *Framing the Nation: Languages of 'Modernity' in India* (Calcutta: Seagull Books, 2011).

Srinivas, S. V., *Megastar: Chiranjeevi and Telugu Cinema after N. T. Rama Rao* (New Delhi: Oxford University Press, 2009).

Srivastava, P., 'Mature and Marvellous: Madhuri Dixit Is Silencing the Cynics Who Feel There's No Place for Older Actresses in B-Town', *Daily Mail* 10 August 2013, <http://www.dailymail.co.uk/indiahome/indianews/article-2388855/Madhuri-Dixit-silencing-cynics-feel-theres-place-older-actresses-B-Town.html> (accessed 29 December 2016).

Sud, S., 'Foxy Lady Trailed & Nailed!', *Cine Blitz* October 1990, pp. 84–7.

Sundaram, S., 'Queen of (He)arts', *Movie* June 1996, pp. 32–7.

Thomas, R., *Bombay before Bollywood: Film City Fantasies* (New Delhi: Orient Blackswan, 2014).

Thomas, R., *Bombay before Bollywood: Film City Fantasies* (Albany: State University of New York Press, 2015).

Travasso, A., 'The Front-Runners of the Nineties', *Showtime* May 1990, pp. 36–7, 43–5.

Turner, G., 'The Economy of Celebrity', in S. Redmond and S. Holmes (eds), *Stardom and Celebrity: A Reader* (Los Angeles, CA and London: Sage Publications, 2007), pp. 193–205.

Uberoi, P., 'Imagining the Family: An Ethnography of Viewing Hum Aapke Hain Koun …!', in R. Dwyer and C. Pinney (eds), *Pleasure and the Nation: The Politics and Consumption of Popular Culture in India* (Delhi: Oxford University Press, 2000), pp. 309–36.

Virdi, J., *The Cinematic ImagiNation: Indian Popular Film as Social History* (New Brunswick, NJ., and London: Rutgers University Press, 2003).

Vitali, V., 'The Families of Hindi Cinema: A Socio-Historical Approach to Film Studies', *Framework: The Journal of Cinema and Media* vol. 42 (2000), <http://www.frameworknow.com/vol-42> (accessed 13 November 2016).

Walavalkar, V., *Screen* 8 February 1991, p. 14.

Wilkinson-Weber, C., *Fashioning Bollywood: The Making and Meaning of Hindi Film Costume* (London and New York: Bloomsbury, 2014).

FILMOGRAPHY

ABODH/INNOCENT (Hiren Nag, India, 1984), Gauri

AWARA BAAP/VAGRANT FATHER (Sohanlal Kanwar, India, 1985), Barkha

SWATI (Kranthi Kumar, India, 1986), Anandi

MANAV HATYA/MURDER OF MEN (Sudarshan K. Rattan, India, 1986), Rama

HIFAZAT/PROTECT (Prayag Raj, India, 1987), Janki

UTTAR DAKSHIN/NORTH SOUTH (Prabhat Khanna, India, 1987), Chanda

MOHRE/PIECES (Raghuvir Kul, India, 1987), Maya

KHATRON KE KHILADI/DAREDEVILS (T. Rama Rao, India, 1988), Kavita

DAYAVAAN/MERCIFUL (Feroz Khan, India, 1988), Neela

TEZAAB/ACID (N. Chandra, India, 1988), Mohini

VARDI/UNIFORM (Umesh Mehra, India, 1989), Jaya (guest appearance)

ILAAKA/NEIGHBOURHOOD (Aziz Sejawal, India, 1989), Vidya

PREM PRATIGYAA/PROMISE OF LOVE (Bapu, India, 1989), Laxmi

TRIDEV/TRINITY (Rajiv Rai, India, 1989), Divya

KANOON APNA APNA/PERSONAL LAW (B. Gopal, India, 1989), Bharathi

PARINDA/PIGEON (Vidhu Vinod Chopra, India, 1989), Paro

PAAP KA ANT/END OF SIN (Vijay Reddy, India, 1989), Jyoti

RAM LAKHAN (Subhash Ghai, India, 1989), Radha

MUJRIM/CRIMINAL (Umesh Mehra, India, 1989), Sonia

MAHA SANGRAM/EPIC STRUGGLE (Mukul Anand, India, 1990), Jhumri

DIL/HEART (Indra Kumar, India, 1990), Madhu

JEEVAN EK SANGHURSH/LIFE IS A STRUGGLE (Rahul Rawail, India, 1990), Madhu
SAILAAB/FLOOD (Deepak Balraj Vij, India, 1990), Dr. Sushma Malhotra
JAMAI RAJA/SON-IN-LAW (A. Kodandarami Reddy, India, 1990), Rekha
THANEDAAR/JAILER (Raj N. Sippy, India, 1990), Chanda
PYAAR KA DEVTA/GOD OF LOVE (K. Bapaiah, India, 1990), Radha
KISHEN KANHAIYA (Rakesh Roshan, India, 1990), Anju
IZZATDAAR/THE HONOURABLE ONE (K. Bapaiah and J. Hemambar, India, 1990), Mohini
DEEWANA MUJH SA NAHIN/NO ONE AS CRAZY AS ME (Y. Nageshwar Rao, India, 1990), Anita
KHILAAF/AGAINST (Rajeev Nagpaul, India, 1991), Sweta
PRATIKAR/RETRIBUTION (Rama Rao Tatineni, India, 1991), Madhu
SAAJAN/LOVER (Lawrence D'Souza, India, 1991), Pooja Saxena
PRAHAAR: THE FINAL ATTACK (Nana Patekar, India, 1991), Shirley
100 DAYS (Partho Ghosh, India, 1991), Devi
KHEL/SPORT (Rakesh Roshan, India, 1992), Seema
ZINDAGI EK JUAA/LIFE IS A GAMBLE (Prakash Mehra, India, 1992), Juhi Singh
SANGEET/SONG (K. Vishwanath, India, 1992), Nirmala/Sangeeta
PREM DEEWANE/CRAZY LOVE (Sachin, India, 1992), Shivangi Mehra
DHARAVI (Sudhir Mishra, India, 1992), Dream girl (guest appearance)
BETA/SON (Indra Kumar, India, 1992), Saraswati
DIL TERA AASHIQ/HEART IS YOUR LOVER (Lawrence D'Souza, India, 1993), Sonia Khanna/Savitri
SAHIBAAN (Ramesh Talwar, India, 1993), Sahibaan
PHOOL/FLOWER (Singeetham Srinivasa Rao, India, 1993), Guddi
KHALNAYAK/VILLAIN (Subhash Ghai, India, 1993), Ganga/Gangotri Devi
AASOO BANE ANGAAREY/TEARS BECOME BURNING COALS (Mehul Kumar, India, 1993), Usha
ANJAAM/CONSEQUENCE (Rahul Rawail, India, 1994), Shivani Chopra
HUM AAPKE HAIN KOUN ...!/WHO AM I TO YOU ...! (Sooraj R. Barjatya, India, 1994), Nisha Choudhury

YARAANA/FRIENDSHIP (David Dhawan, India, 1995), Lalita/Shikha
RAJA/KING (Indra Kumar, India, 1995), Madhu Garewal
PAAPPI DEVATAA/SINFUL GOD (Harmesh Malhotra, India, 1995), Reshma
RAJKUMAR/PRINCE (Pankaj Parashar, India, 1996), Rajkumari Vishaka
PREM GRANTH/BOOK OF LOVE (Rajiv Kapoor, India, 1996), Kajri
KOYLA/COAL (Rakesh Roshan, India, 1997), Gauri
MAHAANTA: THE FILM/GREAT ONE (Afzal Khan, India, 1997), Jenny
DIL TO PAGAL HAI/THE HEART IS CRAZY (Yash Chopra, India, 1997), Pooja
MOHABBAT/ROMANCE (Reema Rakesh Nath, India, 1997), Shweta Sharma
MRITYUDAND/DEATH SENTENCE (Prakash Jha, India, 1997), Ketki
GHARWALI BAHARWALI/INSIDER OUTSIDER (David Dhawan, India, 1998), guest appearance
WAJOOD/EXISTENCE (N. Chandra, India, 1998), Apoorva Choudhury
AARZOO/DESIRE (Lawrence D'Souza, India, 1999), Pooja Nath
PUKAR/CALL (Rajkumar Santoshi, India, 2000), Anjali
GAJA GAMINI/ELEPHANT (M. F. Husain, India, 2000), Gaja/Gamini/Sangita/Shakuntala
YEH RAASTE HAIN PYAAR KE/THIS ROAD TO LOVE (Deepak S. Shivdasani, India, 2001), Neha
LAJJA/SHAME (Rajkumar Santoshi, India, 2001), Janki
DEVDAS (Sanjay Leela Bhansali, India, 2002), Chandramukhi
HUM TUMHARE HAIN SANAM/I AM YOURS, MY LOVE (K. S. Adhiyaman, India, 2002), Radha
AAJA NACHLE/COME DANCE! (Anil Mehra, India, 2007), Dia Srivastav
YEH JAWAANI HAI DEEWANI/THIS YOUTHFULNESS IS CRAZY (Ayan Mukherjee, India, 2013), Mohini (guest appearance)
DEDH ISHQIYA/ONE AND A HALF ROMANCE (Abhishek Chaubey, India, 2014), Begum Para
GULAAB GANG/PINK GANG (Soumik Sen, India, 2014), Rajjo
BUCKET LIST (Tejas Vijay Deoskar, India, 2018), Madhura Sane

INDEX

List of Illustrations

While considerable effort has been made to correctly identify the copyright holders, this has not been possible in all cases. We apologise for any apparent negligence and any omissions or corrections brought to our attention will be remedied in any future editions.

PUBLISHED TITLES

Amitabh Bachchan *Sunny Singh*
Brigitte Bardot *Ginette Vincendeau*
Julie Christie *Melanie Bell*
Penelope Cruz *Ann Davies*
Rock Hudson *John Mercer*
Deborah Kerr *Sarah Street*
Nicole Kidman *Pam Cook*
Tony Leung Chiu-Wai *Mark Gallagher*
James Mason *Sarah Thomas*
Carmen Miranda *Lisa Shaw*
Mickey Rourke *Keri Walsh*
Hanna Schygulla *Ulrike Sieglohr*
Barbara Stanwyck *Andrew Klevan*
Elizabeth Taylor *Susan Smith*
Denzel Washington *Cynthia Baron*
Natalie Wood *Rebecca Sullivan*
Star Studies *Martin Shingler*

FORTHCOMING

George Clooney *Paul McDonald*